To my good

Steve Danyluk
July 2021

My Fortunate Immigrant Life

My Fortunate Immigrant Life

STEVEN DANYLUK

Deeds Publishing | Athens

Copyright © 2021 — Steven Danyluk

ALL RIGHTS RESERVED—No part of this book may be reproduced in any form or by any electronic or mechanical means, including information storage and retrieval systems, without permission in writing from the authors, except by a reviewer who may quote brief passages in a review.

Published by Deeds Publishing in Athens, GA
www.deedspublishing.com

Printed in The United States of America

Cover design by Mark Babcock.

On the cover: Photo of my mom, Mary, me (in the middle) and Dmytro at a train window on our way to Bremerhaven and the US.

ISBN 978-1-950794-45-4

Books are available in quantity for promotional or premium use. For information, email info@deedspublishing.com.

First Edition, 2021

10 9 8 7 6 5 4 3 2 1

To all the people that contributed to my fortunate life

Contents

Preface	ix
Introduction	xi
Historical Perspective, c. 1945	xi
My Family's Connection to Galicia	xiv
Part 1	
A Brief Description of My Family Genealogy	1
More Details of my Genealogy	5
My Babcha	9
My Mom	11
Escaping the Fighting in 1944	17
After the War in Germany, 1945-1950	21
Coping in Germany After the War	25
Memories of Life in the DP Camps	29
Some Additional Information about Displaced Persons Camps	31
Processing for Emigration to the US	41
More on Emigration processing	45
Sponsorship of the Kunitsky Family	47
An Improbable Circumstance	53
Crossing Over	59
Part 2	
New York in the 1950's	69

Some Historical Details of the Neighborhood	77
Childhood on 7th Street	83
Growing up in the Neighborhood	89
St. George School	101
Some more details of St. George School	109
My Brother Dmytro	113
John and Nick	117
Mary	119
Pre-teens on 1st Avenue	123
Stress on First Avenue	127
Realities of Living in an Apartment	129
Cultural Changes in the 50's and early 60's	131
Teenage Friends	135
Life on 12th Street and High School Years	137
High School Years and New Horizons	141
Drum Corp Years	145

Part 3

My High School Years	149
Another lucky break	153
Work Experience During High School and After Graduation	157
Pre-Marriage	159
Marriage	165
More on My Environment in the 1960s	173
The Joan Toggitt Period	175
The Rumstich Family	179

Frank and Lee Moon	181
On the Road to Academia	183
Some Interesting Anecdotes while in Newark, Delaware	187
Graduate School and Beyond, 1968-1969	193
Afterword	**197**
My last 40 Years	198
Acknowledgements	**201**
About the Author	**203**
References	**205**

Preface

I am the son of Ukrainian farmers who fled their home in western Ukraine in 1944, running west to escape the fighting between the Germans and the Soviets, near the end of WWII. After the war, my family spent five years as displaced persons in the American sector of Germany. My parents refused to be repatriated after the war and after my father died in one of the camps, my mother and my father's mother spent years working towards emigrating to the US. I was born in one such Displaced Persons Camp in Bavaria in 1945, six months after the end of the Second World War, and our family emigrated to the US in 1950 after a series of improbable yet fortunate events. The five years I lived in Germany as a displaced person shaped my life; my struggles with the consequences of losing my father, a chaotic home life in New York City, and assimilation to a US citizen. Improbable good fortune played into my family's survival in a devastated Europe, emigration to America and to me personally, in meeting individuals that contributed to success in my personal and professional life. My life turned a critical corner when I entered high school, met other Americans who were one or more generations ahead of me in assimilation, and met my future wife and her family who provided the initial support for me to transition to becoming an American. Who could have imagined that I would end up in the US, survive growing up in lower Manhattan, receive a PhD in Engineering, and have a successful career as an academic and entrepreneur. This memoir describes some of my early history and the good fortune I experienced in this journey.

In assembling this memoir, I have come to realize how fortunate I have been to be born into the second half of the twentieth century where there have been no major world wars, advances in science and engineering that have made life unbelievingly livable, and where medical technology has created an environment free of many of the diseases that have plagued prior generations. My history of the twentieth century is part of a picture-puzzle where the puzzle pieces are snippets of my memory and that of my siblings, as well as historical facts aligned with my life. My intention in writing this memoir is to put together these puzzle pieces and allow my family to get a better sense of how I got to be who I am.

Introduction

Historical Perspective, c. 1945

I arrived in the US with my mother, older sister Mary, and younger brother Dmytro in December 1950 on the USS General Muir, an army transport ship operated by the Army Transport Organization, after approximately a 12-day trip across the Atlantic. My father's mother, Rosalia, was initially part of our family group escaping the war front, but joined up with us in New York about a month later. We, perhaps, were the last group of displaced persons stranded in Aschaffenburg, a Displaced Persons camp in Bavaria, at the end of WWII, in the US Zone of Occupation, and were the last to emigrate to the US as part of the immigration laws passed by Congress. We were literally deposited in Manhattan, at approximately 42nd Street and the Hudson River, with immigration processing having been done at Bremerhaven, our departure point in Germany. This was the start of my life as an immigrant and assimilation to a US citizen. This beginning had a profound influence on my life. I was born into a Ukrainian culture, lost my father to a heart attack in Germany and transitioned to that of an American in the largest city in the US. Along the way, I have gone through a lot of anxiety, growing up without a father, coping with being an immigrant and, assimilation into the American culture. Over my life, I have told many people, including my daughters, various bits and pieces of my early history but I had never organized this history, even in my own mind, into a coherent whole. I have, therefore, decided to write this all out so that my children and their children would have a record of my history and know how I became who I am.

In the last several years I have focused on thinking through the various facts that I remember from my childhood and trying to place these within my life. Reconstructing the seventy-odd years of my life has taken a good deal of wringing of my memory, and in some cases anxiety, speaking with and comparing notes with my siblings, and researching the history of the 20th century. I believe that to understand anyone's life, one needs to understand how the person fits within the framework of history and in my case especially, how my mother and father coped with the world wars of the twentieth century. I am starting these memoirs with this in mind, and beginning with some historical background of my family's heritage.

I was born in December 1945 in Lower Franconia in Bavaria and spent five years there in a Displaced Persons camp, and while I remember some details of my life in Bavaria, many are vague memories which I have had to jar out of my subconscious or research through readings, or discussions with my siblings.

When my family and I arrived in the US, we lived on the lower east side of Manhattan in the vicinity of St. George Catholic Church, which is located on East 7th Street, between 2nd Avenue and the Bowery. This neighborhood was populated by Ukrainians that came from the western part of Ukraine called Galicia (Halychyna in Ukrainian) and was Catholic of the Byzantine Slavonic Rite. St. George Church was partly responsible for helping my family, as well as other families, to get to New York, and many of these families settled in the immediate vicinity of the church. Each of these identifiers such as having Galicia as the homeland, living on the lower east side of Manhattan, the Bowery, and Catholicism have shaped my life. In my childhood and pre-teens, I was aware of the peculiarities of my surroundings, especially of living in a community where Ukrainian was spoken by almost everyone including strangers in the streets, schools, restaurants, doctors, and the shop store proprietors. Even the funeral home, Peter Jarema's, was part of the Ukrainian community. And although I exclusively spoke Ukrainian at home as I was growing up, I tried to distance myself from my Ukrainian heritage and spoke only English in the streets. It took years for me to stop translating English into Ukrainian and vice-versa, and to stop using 'Thou' and 'Thee' when I spoke to any adult, but which I continued doing with my grandmother and mother, until they died.

To provide some examples of what I mean by 'the person fits within the framework of history' I give you the following: my grandmother talked fondly of Austrians and the Grand Duke Ferdinand whose assassination precipitated WWI. I understand, to a certain extent, Polish, and many of my friends in the Ukrainian neighborhood of Manhattan had surnames that sounded Polish, and my mother's, father's and grandmother's birth certificates lists their nationality as Polish. We were made to understand, even as children, that we were a small religious minority of Catholics, different from the Orthodox Ukrainians living in the same vicinity of New York. These Orthodox Ukrainians emigrated from the larger part of Ukraine that was dominated by Russian Orthodoxy. We were taught to stay away from these Ukrainians as well as the Poles. How are all of these bits of information related? This is the question that I have come to examine these past few years. I dug into these facts as a research problem, probing my memory, speaking with my siblings, and reading historical accounts. In this process, however, my unearthing of facts of my life has re-opened stressful and even painful memories which I had never before confronted or related to anyone. I have also come to appreciate the many turns of fate and good fortune I have had throughout my life.

I will begin my memoir by describing some historical facts that explain the first question I've stated above: How did my family ended up with an Austrian/Polish connection when they had not moved from their plot of land for many generations, how my family, and eventually I, ended up in Germany, in a Displaced Persons camp and emigrated to the US.

My Family's Connection to Galicia

As I've said above, my family are from western Ukraine in a region called Galicia, more specifically eastern Galicia that abuts the Carpathian Mountains on its south-western border and, the larger-part of Ukraine. Ukraine has a history going back to 1000CE but since the 1730s the greater part of Ukraine was governed by Russia. The western part of Ukraine, Galicia, was ruled by the Austro-Hungarian Empire until the beginning of the First World War, and was subdivided into eastern and western regions (as you look on a map with the north pole at the top of the page). Galicia sat at the border between the Austro-Hungarian Empire, Poland, and Russia, and each of these countries and empires tried to incorporate Galicia into its territory. The Danyluk side of the family came from a small village, Bodnariv, in the orbit of the major city of Stanislaviv (re-named Ivano Frankivsk by the Soviets in 1962) just east of the border that separates western and eastern Galicia. Although Galicia was ruled by Austria-Hungary since the eighteenth century, both the western and eastern parts were administered by Poland with the approval of Austria-Hungary up to the beginning of the First World War.

Figure 1. Map of Eastern Europe showing the partitions of Poland by Russia. Obtained from Massi's book. Note that Poland, turned over to Russia in the Second Partition, was in control of that part of Ukraine in which my family resided, at the southern portion of this region, near the River Bug.

Both eastern and western Galicia went back and forth between the Austro-Hungarian Empire and Russia since the early 1770's, and Poland when it was taken over by Russia during the reign of Catherine the Great (see books by Massie and Kochanski). The 'western' part of Galicia intrudes into and sits on the border with Poland, Czechoslovakia and Hungary and the 'eastern' side abuts the historical border of Ukraine which for many centuries was occupied and ruled by Russia. Austria-Hungary was an empire composed of semi-autonomous principalities which were given the freedom to use local languages and prescribe and enforce their own laws. With the permission of Austria-Hungary, western Galicia in the late 19th century was formally incorporated into Poland but eastern Galicia was continually argued over into the 20th century. It was turned over to Polish administration by the Austro-Hungarian Empire prior to WWI, although the Austro-Hungarian empire did not cede control of this region. My family's small plot of land was located in eastern Galicia and came under the administration of Poland. From what I have read, the population of eastern Galicia was populated by Poles and Ukrainians, with many of the towns and cities containing large fractions of Jews that lived 'beyond the pale' in relation to Moscow. World War I caused many of the traditional borders to be shifted or obliterated, and the Ottoman and Austro-Hungarian empires to be broken up into new countries. The Ottoman Empire lost the Arab lands in the middle East, this was the time of Lawrence of Arabia, and the Austro-Hungarians lost Galicia. Furthermore, the Bolsheviks wanted a buffer between themselves and Germany, while Poland wanted to reconstruct their previous kingdom prior to partition by Russia. After WWI, the various territories, especially those in eastern Europe and especially Galicia, were vigorously argued over by Poland and the Bolsheviks, while the United States insisted that it would not support the territorial expansion of the winners of the war, such as Bolshevik Russia, at the expense of the losers of the war, Germany and Austria-Hungary. At the insistence of Woodrow Wilson, the Treaty of Versailles (19 June 1919) stipulated that eastern European nations sign the 'Minorities Treaty' where the signatories would ensure "…full and complete protection of life and liberty to all inhabitants…without distinction of birth, nationality, language, race or religion" (see the book by Baker). This meant that local minorities that were left stateless when the Austro-Hungarian empire was broken up, would not be annexed without their consent by Soviet Russia, England or France. It was assumed that whole swats of land, with a preponderance of a given nationality, could be formed into nations, as a result of a plebiscite. This concept was especially important to Galicia, since under Polish rule, with a significant Ukrainian population, Ukraine hoped to establish itself as a nation that included Galicia. Galicia had a mix of Polish, Jewish and Ukrainian populations, therefore it was not easy to decide how to apportion the lands, assigning the land to Poland or recognizing an expanded Ukrainian nation. Since Russia was one of the victors of WWI, it wanted Galicia to be ceded to it, the rationale being that a large portion of the population spoke Ukrainian, a Slavic language. Apparently, there was no political will to create a separate Ukrainian nation, or incorporate Galicia within the larger Ukraine, but an agreement was sought to establish a boundary separating the Ukrainians and Poles. There was serious disagreement between the Entente Powers as to where to fix the boundaries of Poland with respect to Ukraine because of the intermixing of nationalities and ethnicities. In any event, the Bolshevik and Polish governments wanted to annex Galicia but the Entente Powers, England and France, and especially Woodrow Wilson, pushed for the idea of self-determination as the criterion as to where the dividing line would be between Bolshevik and Polish lands. As a result, western Galicia was assigned to Poland and eastern Galicia went back and forth between Russia and Poland-finally being claimed by Poland without agreement of Russia-and this assignment of land depended on the outcome of further negotiations at the Peace Conference. All of this occurred at the Peace Conference in 1919-1921, and Eastern Galicia came under Polish rule until 1939. Western Galicia called 'Kresy' by the Poles-a name I first learned when reading the book by Kochanski (see the reference)-is listed on my mothers' birth certificate (Kreis as it is spelled there) as her region of birth, and Polish as her nationality, because she was born in 1923 at the time when both Western and Eastern Galicia were deemed Polish. It is this history of the lead-up to the First World War, the time after and between the world wars, and WWII, that I remember hearing about from my fraternal Grandmother, Rosalia, or Babcha as we called her, and various history I learned in the Ukrainian school in NYC where I grew up.

Figure 2. Map of Eastern Europe showing the location of Galicia, with the inset showing the eastern and western portions (obtained from Subtelny's book, p. 246).

Bear with me a little longer as I conclude this brief historical account of Galicia because you can't understand my family background without this knowledge. Galicia was divided into an eastern and western parts, both parts ruled by Poland but the eastern part was in dispute.

As stated above, the Treaty of Versailles stipulated that eastern Galicia was to be transferred to Soviet Russia following agreement of a yet to be determined artificial boundary (the Curzon Line) that divided disputed territories of Poland and Russia. The adults in the Ukrainian community where I grew up lived through this era when their land was in dispute and culture was suppressed and, therefore, resented both the Poles and the Soviet Russians. This resentment and bad feeling carried over into Manhattan and was instilled in us youngsters as we were growing up. This dispute by the Entente Powers as to the location of the territorial demarcation (Curzon) line veered east of Lviv (known at one time as Lemberg in German and Lwow in Polish) and ended just 130 km southeast from my family's ancestral home i.e. my family came to be in Polish territory. The Curzon line location was subsequently corrected to include Lviv into western Galicia (note line A and line B on the map) and although the location of the Curzon line in itself didn't affect my family directly, its discussion and location confused the ethnicities of the local population, and of course, that of my family. The next-to-last changeover of Galicia occurred in another 'minor' war, in 1921, between Poland and the Bolsheviks, ending with the Poles being victorious. The war was ended with the Treaty of Riga (note the document in google ungarisches-institut.de/dokumente/pdf/19210318-1.pdf) signed on 8 March 1921, that settled the eastern border of Poland and incorporated parts of it between Soviet Russia and Poland. This new boundary was different but similar to the Curzon line, and included Stanislaviv, the major city near where my parents lived, within Polish territory. Therefore, my family was in Poland and my mother's place of birth is listed as Poland just after WWI, since she was born in 1923. The last change of this region occurred when Eastern Galicia was agreed to be Polish as a result of the Molotov-Ribbentrop Agreement of 1939, one of the bizarre secret treaties signed by Germany and Russia just prior to WWII. After the Soviets joined the Allies in the fight against Hitler, Stalin pressed Churchill and Roosevelt in their meetings in Quebec, Teheran and Yalta near the end of WWII in 1944, to transfer Galicia to Soviet Ukrainian rule, closely following the original Curzon line to delineate the boundaries of Poland and the Soviet Union. So, my family ended up in Soviet Ukraine, just prior to their escape, near the end of 1944.

To briefly review what I have written above, Galicia was Austro-Hungarian until WWI, then Polish in 1919, then finally Soviet in 1944. It seems astounding to me how world events such as the world wars, the breakup of empires, the demarcation of borders by an artificial border such as the Curzon Line written into the Paris Peace Accord, and the Molotov-Ribbentrop secret agreement which redrew the boundaries of Poland and the Soviet Union in 1939, and the annexation of this land by Soviet Ukraine in 1944, all affected my family and eventually my life. I'll leave it to you to read about the world wars and the shifting of borders in this region of the world since it is beyond the scope of my memoir to get into these details.

I had learned some of this history (see the book by Subtelny and Goldbaum listed in the references) leading up to WWI, and the interwar years up to WWII, by reading history books, and I recall hearing part of this history from my grandmother. For example, I recall, in childhood, my Babcha telling me stories of Franz Joseph, the Austrian emperor, the famines in the region in which she lived in 1921 after WWI, the famines in Ukraine in 1931 and 1933 (called Holodomor by the Ukrainians), how she tried to use her connection to Austria, since, it turns out, she was the daughter of an Austrian, as a way to leave her village during WWII under the protection of the Germans, and travel into Germany to get away from the (Ukrainian and Russian) Soviets as they pushed to regain 'Soviet' territory. It now makes sense to me that my grandmother had a special affinity for the Austrians, that we children were taught to dislike the Poles and Russians and, that we wound up in Germany near the end of WWII, presumably because of this Austrian connection. Without this connection, I never would have ended up in the US.

My Fortunate Immigrant Life

Part 1

A Brief Description of My Family Genealogy

The enclosed family tree of Figure 3, prepared by my older sister Mary, shows both the Danyluk (my father's side) and Kowalchuk (my mother's side) sides of my family. I was told the following by my sister: my maternal grandfather Dmytro Kowalchuk served in World War I and when he returned from the war, he settled in a village named Wysochanka. He married Matrona Zanek and he and my grandmother had two children, Johanna, my mother, and Gregory. Dmytro was a farmer and thatched-roof maker and raised an orchard of cherries. Matrona and Dmytro were poor, too poor to buy windows for their cottage, so oiled paper was used instead of glass as the window panes. Their son Gregory, my Mom's brother, was supposedly very smart but was not allowed go to school because he was needed to help on the farm.

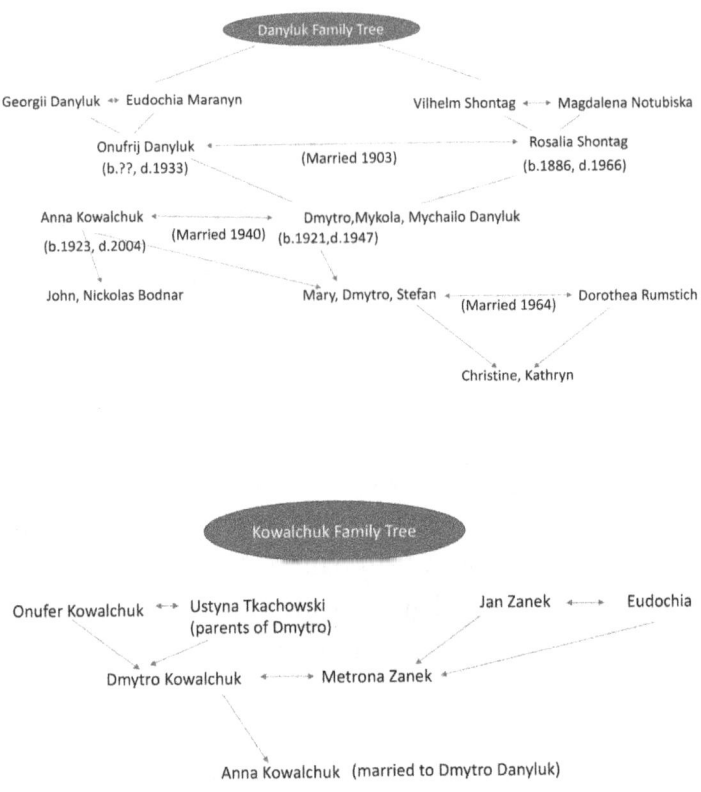

Figure 3. Geneology maps of the Kowalchuk and Danyluk sides of the family.

On the Danyluk side of the genealogy, my grandmother's parents, Magdalena Notubiska was married to Wilhelm Shoentag. They had many children-one of them, the youngest, was Rosalia, who was my fraternal grandmother, known by me as Babcha, and who I write about in this memoir. Rosalia married Onufrij Danyluk, and they had eight children but only three males survived to adulthood: Mychailo, Mykola and Dmytro, my father. My dad, Dmytro, her youngest son, married Johanna Kowalchuk, my mother who went by the name of Anna, and they had three children: Mary, my older sister, me, and Dmytro my younger brother. My father, Dmytro, died in Germany in 1947. It was we children, my mother Anna, and mother-in-law Rosalia, who emigrated to the US in 1950. Anna met Wasyl Bodnar in New York City in1953, never married him, but had two children with him, John and Nicholas Bodnar. I married Dorothea Rumstich in 1964 and we have two daughters, Christine and Kathryn.

More Details of my Genealogy

My fathers' mother, Rosalia, Babcha as we called her, was born in 1886 in Bodnariv, when Galicia was the eastern border of the Austro-Hungarian empire. As I've already mentioned, my grandmother had good things to say of Franz Joseph and Franz Ferdinand. She talked fondly of the emperor and told us grandchildren that she was very sad when he died. She was 26 years old at the time of his assassination. Austrians lived in Galicia either as military soldiers or as administrative or support staff who oversaw this remote part of the empire, and in the process, this inter-mixing of the Austrians with the local population led to the mixture of the nationalities. It is through this intermixing that my grandmother's father was an Austrian named, Vilhelm Shoentag, (with an umlaut over the o) who was a blacksmith, most likely working in support of the Austrian army. My Babcha's mother, Magdelena Notubitska, was a housewife, who's maiden name sounds of Polish origin. As I've said above, this region of Ukraine had a mix of Poles, and Ukrainians so it is not surprising that Polish and Austrian names crept into many families. I have read on Wikipedia that there were three sizable ethnicities in this region: a Jewish population of about 20%, with the rest divided between the Poles and Ukrainians. The proportion of Jews is not surprising since Galicia, Poland, and Belarus, were considered beyond the 'pale,' i.e.

that region beyond Moscow where Jews were permitted to live by the Czar. My grandma was married to Onufrij Danyluk in 1903 and he died when my father was about 11 years old. Babcha, in her 50s, married her second husband, by the last name of Hawryluk, whose first name I do not know, and he died in 1942 just before my sister Mary was born. For reasons that I don't understand, my Babcha went back to the name of Danyluk after her second husband died, and Mary speculates that Babcha's second marriage may not have been recorded. My Babcha and my mother's family, the Kowalchuks, continued to live on their plots of land in Galicia throughout the First and Second World Wars until 1944 when it seemed inevitable that the Soviets would win and the Germans lose the war. During and between the world wars and as a result of my Babcha staying put, she traded her small farm in Bodnariv for a larger one in Victoriv when the local population was escaping the world wars and were willing to sell their farms to their neighbors at bargain basement prices. She apparently traded three plots of land in Bodnariv and bought a contiguous plot of land in Victoriv. Both these small villages, just two miles apart, were in the orbit of Stanislaviv, the capitol of the county (Oblast), situated about 130 kilometers southeast of the major city of Lviv. Stanislaviv was renamed as Ivano-Frankivsk in 1962 by Nikita Krushchev in honor of a famous Ukrainian poet, Ivan Franko. I have been told by Mary that Babcha bore eight children, five of whom died in infancy or early childhood. The three sons who were Danyluks survived to adulthood, married and had children: the eldest Mykola (d. 1941), the middle son Mychailo (d. 1944), and my father Dmytro, the youngest, who was born in 1921 and died in 1947. Mary tells me that Babcha spoke with grief of a daughter, Marika, that died at five years old, a fact that she never got over.

Figure 4. An Immigration passport photo of my Babcha when she was approximately 60 years old.

Both of my uncles as well as my father died as a result of WWII: Babcha told us children how Mychailo was killed in 1944 by Soviet army partisans. Mykola, my other uncle, who left his home in 1945 to run an errand by riding a bicycle through a forest near their home, was never heard from again. My father survived these war years until 1947. As I've already mentioned, my mother and father had three children, Mary (b. 1942), me (b.1945) and Dmytro (b.1947) who was born after my father died. Mary is single and never married, I married Dorothea Rumstich in 1964 and we have two daughters Christine (b.1965) and Kathryn (b.1967). Christine has two children, Emily and Alex, Kathryn also has two children, Avery and Evan. Christine's daughter Emily married Johnathan Cameron and, at the time of this writing, have two children, William (Liam) and Adeline. Alex married Samantha Seay and they have a daughter, Amelia. Dmytro married Faye Wartellski, and have a daughter Jennifer and son James. Jennifer has three children, and James has two sons. Nick married Rosie Acevedo and they have one daughter, Nicole, and two grandchildren. John married but had no children.

My Babcha

If you had met my grandmother you would immediately see that she was a sharp and shrewd woman who survived both world wars through her wits and ingenious tactics. She was the alpha female in our family and everyone including my mother knew to follow her advice and instructions. She told us children how proud she was that she acquired land through wheeling and dealing. I vividly recall her talking about the famines in Ukraine in between the two World Wars, and 1932 and 1933, when Stalin sealed the borders, and ordered grain and other produce shipped to Moscow (see the books by Robert Conquest and Anne Applebaum), leaving little food for the local population. This deliberate policy of Stalin caused millions of Ukrainians to die of starvation. However, at this time, Bodnariv and Victoriv, were under Polish rule because of the Treaty of Riga, therefore it would not have been subject to confiscation of grain and other food stuffs since the confiscation of food occurred in the Russian-controlled Ukraine. Babcha was aware of the famine in greater Ukraine but told us these stories of famine as if it had happened to her and her family. For example, Babcha also told us children how she hid potatoes in the field near her home to prevent either the Poles or the Bolsheviks from confiscating them. She would sneak out in the middle of the night to retrieve these potatoes which the family would then cook and eat at night.

Babcha told these stories of hunger and starvation as a warning to us children of Soviet and German armies confiscating food as they saw fit. Mary and I remember other stories by Babcha; that my father, was abducted by a group of partisans in the winter of 1944, with their intent being to enlist him in their group. He was marched, without boots, in the snow until he fainted and was left for dead. The partisans, who were on horseback, left him and he, somehow, made his way home after a number of days. I also recall hearing about the Whites and Reds (the White pro-monarchy group and Red Bolshevik factions fighting for control of the Soviet Revolution just after 1917) in relation to fighting around her home but I had no idea at that time what she was talking about. These stories indicate how my grandmother worked to keep her family, especially her sons, away from the fighting and that the life in war, especially near the battle fronts, where either army conscripted young boys and men to join their side under penalty of death, had devastating effects. I do not recall mention of her first husband, or of her father. Babcha was illiterate but she knew the value of education and I recall her admonishing my mother in New York to learn to read and write. As an aside, I've also read horrible stories of how the Soviets, during their march west into Poland, would rape women and kill all young boys and men, and take whatever they wanted from the households. If you are interested, and have the stomach for it, you can read more details about this in the book *Bloodlands* by Keith Lowe.

My Mom

My mother, who went by the name of Anna, was christened as Johanna. She was born in 1923 to Dmytro Kowalchuk and Matrona Zanek. My mother talked lovingly of her brother Gregory; about what a good man he was, smart and hard working. Matrona's mother, the grandmother of my mother, was named Eudochia and her maternal grandfather was Jan. Kowalchuk is a traditional Ukrainian name while Zanek sounds to me of Polish origin. My mother's fraternal grandfather was Dnufer Kowalchuk and he was married to Ustyna Tkachowski. My parents were married in Victoriv in 1941, at the time that it was under Polish rule, after the Germans had overrun Poland from the west, and the Soviets from the east. My sister Mary was born (August 1942) shortly after my parents married, when the fighting was at its worst. As was the tradition at the time, this was an arranged marriage and my mother went to live in Babcha's village and home, which was a small thatched-roof cottage sitting on a plot of land that my Babcha farmed. I had seen a home similar to the one occupied by my Babcha, when I visited Ukraine in 1993, to be introduced to my aunt, the wife of my mother's brother. The home still had a thatched roof and root cellar, and a small family cemetery on the property. I have been told the following story by Mary: my mother was apprehensive of the marriage to my father partly because she was just eighteen at the time, and she hid in the attic of her home when my grandma came to visit with my father, to be introduced before the marriage. This introduction did not take place at this time but, after my parents married, they eventually settled on the farm owned by Babcha as WWII was in progress. Recall that Hitler invaded Poland in 1939 and the Barbarossa Campaign (the German push to overrun Soviet Russia) was launched in 1941 as part of Hitler's plan to conquer Ukraine and repopulate it with Germans. My parents married during WWII and continued to farm their land along with Babcha as the Germans pushed into Poland and Ukraine. Both my parents had little formal education; my Dad went through grades 1-6 and my Mom through grades 1-3 which would have been the norm for children of farmers living outside of the major metropolitan centers. You can see from what I have just related that the period of the early and mid-20th century still followed rules of social behavior passed down from the 19th century.

In my research over these past few years I wanted to know how my babcha survived the First World War. By happenstance I came across a book by Peter Englund, *The Beauty and the Sorrow*, which records in personal diary accounts, the experiences of individuals who have gone through the First World War. This is a story of the clash of empires, that of the Astro-Hungarian and Russian Empires, the eastern front of World War 1. It was astounding to me to read snippets of the diary of Pal Kelemen, a 20-year old Austrian Lieutenant Hussar, born in Budapest, as he reached the battle front at Stanislau on Tuesday, 25 August 1914. Although the spelling of Stanislau is different from the one I know as Stanislaviv, there is no doubt it is the same city. Englund quotes from that date in the diary, "It is only when the division reaches Halicz, (this is the town just northwest (approximately 10km) of where Babcha lived) that the illusion that this might merely be a manoeuvre is finally smashed. On the way there they meet fleeing peasants and Jews. The mood in the town is apprehensive and confused and the Russians are said to be not far away". Kelemen goes on to write:

"We sleep in tents. At half-past twelve at night: Alarm! The Russian is before the town. I think everyone is a little frightened. I fling on my clothes and run out to join my platoon. On the road the infantry is standing in ranks. Cannon growls. Rifles are rattling some 500 yards ahead. Motor cars dash down the middle of the highway. The lights of their carbide lamps stream in long rows toward Halicz on the road from Stanislau…When morning dawned, the population was pouring out of the city in long files. On carts, on foot, on horseback. Everyone making shifts to save himself. All of them carrying away what they can. And exhaustion, dust, sweat, panic on every face, terrible dejection, pain, and suffering. Their eyes are frightened, their movement craven: ghastly terror oppresses them. As if the dust cloud they stirred up has fastened itself to them and could not float away".

Englund continues saying that Kelemen is seeing "the first bloody and confused clashes with the invading Russians" (recall that this part of Ukraine was the eastern border of the Austro-Hungarian Empire) in what later would to be called the Battle of Lemberg (Lviv). This first-hand eyewitness account of Kelemen puts me into the scene of the confrontation of the armies of the Austro-Hungarian Empire and the Russian Empire and I can picture my Babcha, 28 years old at the time, part of the hoard of people fleeing to escape the fighting. I wish that I had talked to her about this particular day in 1914 so that I could know how she escaped being killed.

My immediate family and prior generations were farmers growing food for themselves with the little left over sold in Stanislaviv, approximately 10km (6 miles) southwest from their village. I have read that the peasants in the Austro-Hungarian empire were allowed 14 acres of land and as I've said above, Babcha bought or traded some of this land from families that had decided to escape at various times of war. I'm not sure how many acres she cultivated. I recall hearing that eggs and milk were the goods used for trading with the city population, and that their farm had chickens, a horse and cow, and some hogs. I had heard many times from Babcha and my mother how 'we' were village people and different from the city folk. I recall various tales of farm living; that cow meat was only sparingly eaten and the farmers usually ate chickens and pigs and very seldom beef, unless the cow was too old to give milk or birth a calf. When I was a child in Manhattan we hardly ever ate cow meat, and as we were settling into living like Americans, my mother would sometimes buy a cut of cow meat such as a steak which she would fry in a pan on a gas stove so that it was almost burnt. This is how she learned to cook meat, assuming it came from an old cow, and she never lost this habit. This social divide between the farmers and the city folk also carried over in Manhattan, and because of the closeness of the neighborhood, this caused some awkwardness in the relations between the Ukrainians, because the 'city' folk looked down their noses at the 'peasants.'

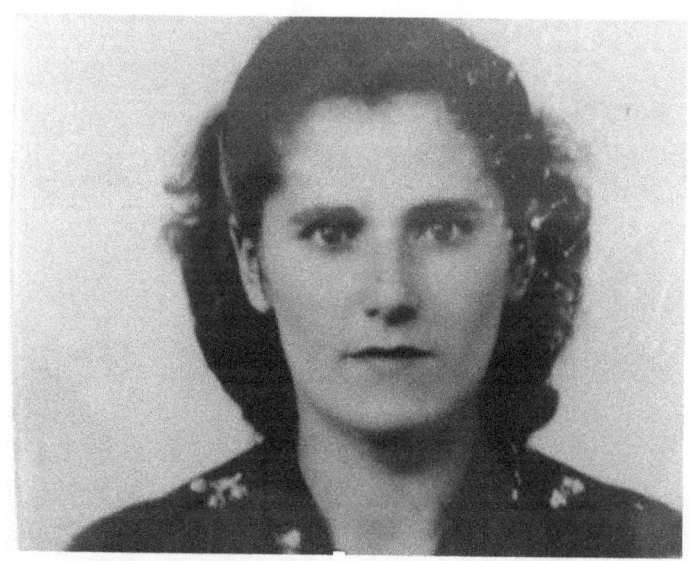

Figure 5. Photo of my mom, most likely passport photo.

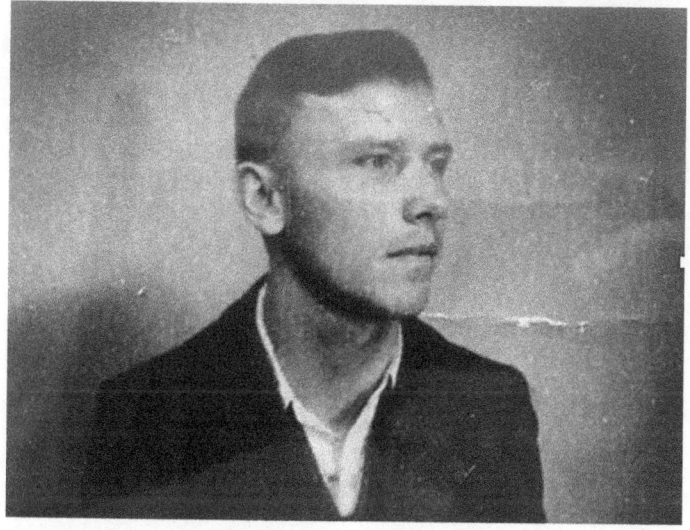

Figure 6. Photo of my dad, most likely passport photo, sometime in the 1940s

Escaping the Fighting in 1944

My family left their village in December of 1944, close to the end of WWII, after the start of D-Day (Operation Overlord), which was on June 6, 1944. I have been told by Mary that the decision to leave their village 1944, was made during the time when the Soviets had overrun Stanislaviv. My dad came home after hearing the news that the Soviet army had ordered scores of Ukrainians exiled to Siberia, and prisoners in the local jail to be taken out into the street and shot, and said that he could not stay in their home any longer, and was leaving. I have assumed since I first heard this story that my dad would leave without the women in his family since he would be the one that would be killed first. Babcha and Mom said they were going with him and this was how the decision was made for the entire family to escape west. I have read that most of the Jews in Stanislaviv were 'lost,' either escaped, sent to Siberia or murdered at this time because many were never heard from again. During that time, the Soviets were pushing west into Galicia and Ukraine after the Germans' Barbarossa campaign stalled west of Kiev. The Ukrainian Soviet forces began their campaign to push the German forces westward on December 24, 1944, just when the local population heard of the Soviets purging Stanislaviv. The war had finally come to meet them where they lived. This decision to leave was what most of the villagers came to as well, so there was a whole swath of population that left together. Most likely the Ukrainians in Galicia did not know of the launch of D-Day and of the likely doom of the Germans, so their reason for leaving their home must have been to escape the death and destruction anticipated when both armies met at this front. Maps of the formation and advance/retreat of the Soviet and German armies show the armies fighting in the region of Halych close to where Babcha and my parents lived (see for example the Atlas of WWII, Richard Natkiel). My family at this time consisted of my grandmother, mother, father and Mary. They picked up their belongings, everything they could carry, and travelled west, on foot, to escape the fighting. Many of the locals tried to negotiate with the Germans for help in escaping the front and the Soviets. As for the Germans, I have read that they were looking for laborers and made arrangements to take conscripts as well as slave laborers to work in Germany. Whether my family signed on as forced/slave labor or willing conscripts is not known to me because my mom and Babcha would not talk about this with us children. As a result, various groups of peoples moved toward the Carpathian Mountains to escape the Soviets. Eventually, many of the refugees boarded trains on the way to Czechoslovakia, and then Germany. My sister and I are a little murky about how and by what means my family left their home except that, during the confusion, my father was separated from my mother and Babcha, and they, with my sister in their arms, walked westward, eventually boarding one such train heading west. The distance from Stanislaviv and the eastern part of Germany, where we eventually ended up, is 1,300 kilometers so they needed transport to cover this distance. Babcha and Mary were further separated from my mother for several months when my mother got off the train to get some coffee and (this is the astounding part) the train took off without her. The family eventually were reunited, near Schweinfurt, after several months. I don't have any information as to what my father or mother did in the months of separation or how they were able to find each other. My babcha and mother never spoke of their reunion or how they avoided being killed. The dates of my birthday suggest that I was conceived near the end of March or early April 1945 so my parents must have been reunited by this time. The civilian groups that departed their villages and Stanislaviv were in Germany for five months, until the surrender of German forces on 8 May 1945.

Figure 7. Map of Galicia (modified from Kopanski's book) showing the location of the Curzon Lines A and B, Lviv, and Stanislaviv.

After the War in Germany, 1945-1950

So far, I have discussed the prelude to my own life, since I was born after my parents were in Germany and the war was over. As I proceed with this memoir I will describe some of the conditions of my family's life in Germany. You'll see that there are many blanks in my knowledge of the conditions of our existence in Germany, and I've had to research accounts of history and stories of others to describe how this life of theirs may have been.

As a prelude to this narrative, it has been and still is very difficult for me to appreciate the death and destruction of the Second World War in spite of all I've read. As I mentioned above, I have some idea of the conditions when my parents left their village, they were frightened on hearing how civilians were treated and soldiers fought or were killed, they must have heard bombings and seen the on-rush of humanity to escape. As to my family, it has been impressed on me that the local civilians just wanted to survive, and migration from their ancestral homeland was the only way to do this. As a result of World War II, there were millions of people killed and millions displaced, including those murdered outright in the Holocaust, who found themselves in foreign countries having seen brutal scenes too horrible to describe. The book *Bloodlands* by Snyder describes a horrible picture of the war and its aftermath, and peoples' reaction to it. I recommend that you read this book if you want to know the details of how civilians coped with the war. I have spent the last several years reading about the Second World War which then took me back to understand the First World War, then back to the Crimean War, the 'Great Game' which was the struggle of Britain and France with Russia for dominance of the trans-Caucasian frontier, Napoleon's march toward Russia, and finally to Catherine the Great. The centuries have been filled with war and death and destruction and it is easy to miss the larger point that the <u>latter</u> half of the 20th has been the most peaceful of the last 500 years of western civilization. Too much information as they say but helpful and informative to me; pieces of my puzzle. Of course, all this reading was to help me to understand my life.

While writing this memoir I have come to realize that the civilian population that experienced the war must have had post-traumatic stress disorder (PTSD), something not yet identified or given a name while I was growing up. This trauma of war shaped everyone's lives; how individuals coped with their experiences and memories, how they raised their kids and how they behaved in society. The immigrant Ukrainian community in Manhattan had gone through the war and had to deal with this trauma. As I look back now, I can recognize evidence of PTSD from the sadness and anxiety in our community, the distress seen in the eyes of the men and women and how they clung together, and looked for escape from stress and strife. What stands out in my memory, even as a young boy, is of men sitting in bars in the middle of the day, and my thinking how sad these men looked, gazing into the mirror at the back of the bar, hair disheveled, oblivious to their surroundings apparently thinking depressing thoughts. This child's view of the Ukrainian men in the community in Manhattan affected my outlook on life and my determination to leave it as soon as possible.

My notion of a memoir has been that it recounts a life in chronological fashion and I have tried doing it this way in the narrative above. But of course, memory doesn't work that way and so I've had to change my approach. I have memories of visual impressions, events and scenes of being in places and situations which I can't exactly place in a specific time order.

My family's journey through Czechoslovakia and into Germany landed us in Schweinfurt where I was born on December 25, 1945 in a Displaced Persons (DP) camp in the American sector of a defeated Germany. I don't have any information as to how my family ended up in this camp, how the Americans identified or organized these displaced peoples at this early date, or what criteria they used in my family's case to take care of us. My mother and Babcha didn't talk to us children about the war or this part of their journey. I presume that all non-Germans self-identified as an ethnic or religious group and agreed to be governed and provided for by the Americans. I don't know if I was born in a hospital since the period between the surrender of the Germans in May and Dec. 25, 1945 was a very short and chaotic time. In any event, my family was in the Schweinfurt camp when I was born and I was named Steven (Stefan in Ukrainian) because Dec. 25 is the feast day of St. Steven. I wasn't given a middle name. The family spent five years subsisting and surviving in five Displaced Persons camps between my birth and our departure from Bremerhaven for the US.

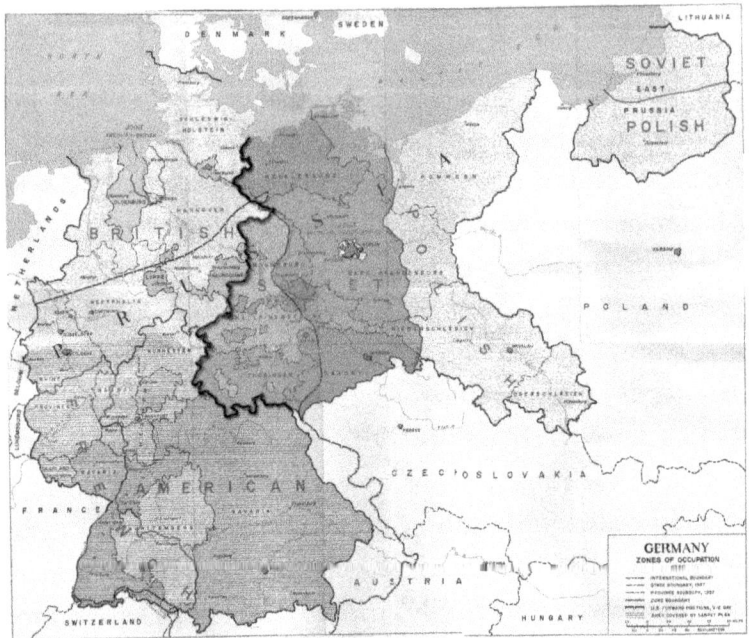

Figure 8. A map of Germany showing the zones of occupation for the British, American, and Soviets after WWII. Note the carved-out region in the northwest, around Bremen that had joint British-American occupancy by mutual agreement, so as to provide sea access to the United States. This map is from Wikipedia. Schweinfurt is located about 50 kilometers due west from the border of Czechoslovakia.

Coping in Germany After the War

Schweinfurt is in Bavaria, a heavily forested region, that was used by the Germans as a place to conduct training of their officers, since it was outside of the bombing pattern of the Allies. The industry in this region was forestry, but eventually the Germans located a ball bearing factory there under cover of the dense forests. I recall Babcha and mom talking about my dad working in forestry but I don't recall any other details, for example, under what conditions he did this work. Near the end of the war, Schweinfurt was heavily bombed by the Allies in an effort to demolish the ball-bearing factory. The civilian population, foreigners as well as Germans, must have continued to run further west to escape this bombing. Mary tells me that, even though she was 4 years old at the time, she remembers the bombing of Schweinfurt, and her fear of the noise and turmoil. You can get the sense of the devastation caused by the fighting from the Internet and YouTube, which shows pictures of the aftereffects of the bombing and fighting in and around Schweinfurt. My family somehow survived the fighting, and luckily this region, including Schweinfurt, ended up in the American zone of occupation, with the Americans assuming the financial responsibility to feed and house the non-German people. Eventually, at the urging of the US, a UN relief agency assumed responsibility to manage, care for and feed the non-German people that were found in Germany. These displaced individuals and families were grouped into Displaced Persons (DP) camps within four zones of occupation under the jurisdiction of the United States, England, France, and the Soviet Union. I'll say more about this agency later. I've enclosed a map of Germany (Figure 8) showing the US zone of occupation with the addition to the American sector being the region around Bremen that is labelled as the American-British region. I point this out because this was where immigrants were processed for entry into the US, and our place of embarkation.

It is hard to grasp the enormity of the scale of death, and the displacement of populations during and after World War II. Besides the dead, there were millions of peoples displaced in Europe and they had no way of getting back to their homeland, or feared the thought of going back. A book by Keith Lowe, *Savage Continent, Europe in the Aftermath of World War II*, describes the shape and look of Europe just after the war, the devastation of the cities and industry, and the lawlessness and desperation of the populations. It is especially distressing to me to read about the moral degradation of the survivors and the vengeance that was perpetrated on the Germans and vice-versa. How my family, especially my father, survived is a mystery to me since millions of men were killed in the war. The United Nations, the Charter for its creation having been signed in October 1945, took responsibility for caring for these people as part of a policy formulated by George Marshall (the person responsible for the Marshall Plan), and this joint partnership between the US and UN resulted in the UN sending personnel to organize the refugees and arrange for their repatriation. The administrators were made up of individuals from the US, France and England and they grouped the DP's according to ethnicity, national origin, or religion.

As another historical aside, I must mention some of the

outcomes of the war. The Allies defeated Germany with joint military forces of England, France and the Soviet Union and, the US entered the war after the Japanese attack on Pearl Harbor. General Eisenhower was the Allied Supreme Commander in Europe as agreed to by Churchill, Stalin and FDR, and eventually oversaw the armistice of the defeated Axis Powers in Europe. As the armistice was enacted, the Allied Control Council took over restoring the economies of Great Britain and France, and the economy and infrastructure of Germany. As you may be aware or you may have read in Churchill's account of WW II, the Soviets quickly pushed into Germany as the war was ending in order to command as much territory as possible and attain hegemony over territory that eventually landed behind the Iron Curtain. The American, French and British forces were aware of the Soviet aims and rushed east. The rapid movement of Patton's 6th army toward Berlin is one example of this. The Allied Powers eventually agreed that Germany would be partitioned along agreed-to lines of demarcation, including the partition of Berlin. There are more details of how these zones were established but in any case, the four major powers were to govern Germany for the foreseeable future. As stated above, during the war, Eisenhower, as Allied Supreme Commander, reported to George Marshall, President Roosevelt's Chief of Staff, who reported to President Roosevelt as the Commander-in-Chief. After the armistice and the death of President Roosevelt on April 12, 1945, Eisenhower was recalled to Washington to become President Truman's Chief of Staff while Marshall became Secretary of State. General Lucius Clay became the military Governor of the US Zone. Clay was charged with the responsibility to keep the peace, house and feed the displaced persons in the American zone, and help steer Germany in a democratic direction. Even though Germany surrendered in 1945, the US was still fighting the Japanese so that troops were expected to be reassigned to the Pacific theatre. When Japan surrendered, the US was anticipating a conflict on the Korean peninsula and this conflict eventually erupted into open hostilities in the mid-1950's. The US government, even in 1945, wanted to discharge its military responsibilities in Europe as soon as possible, but, at the same time, to help in its economic reconstruction, and with the blocking of the Soviet Union from overrunning Europe. I mention this detail because with the haste of the US to discharge its duties in Europe, the displaced persons needed to be repatriated, as soon as possible. As a result, the US committed to an economic plan, the Marshall Plan, and established an immigration policy, to accomplish this. It is the immigration policy that eventually got me to the US. I suggest you read the biography of George Marshall, the reference of which is given in the bibliography below, to get more details of this situation. In any event, the UN and US commitments saved millions of peoples from starvation and death.

My family was one of those displaced families stranded in Germany, fortuitously in the American sector, and were housed, fed and shuttled between five refugee camps between 1945 and 1950, under the general supervision of the United Nations Relief and Repatriation Agency (UNRRA), the group working with the US army. The UNRRA was sponsored by the United Nations but the US and the American Red Cross provided the resources. Our first camp was in Schweinfurt, later transferring to Aschaffenburg, then Phortsheim, Ludwigsburg and Bremen as we went through emigration processing to the US.

Memories of Life in the DP Camps

Obviously, my memories of Germany would have been imprinted after I was approximately 3 years old at best, and I do remember snippets of my five years of life, especially in Aschaffenburg. For example, two of my earliest memories while at one of the DP camps are traumatic; being pecked about my head and face by a long-necked, white goose who stood about as tall as I, and, the draining of the blood from a butchered hog where the hog is hanging by a rope tied to one of its hind leg(s), with throat cut and bleeding into a bucket, while two men stand near and wait for the blood to finish draining. I also remember coming into contact with American soldiers and begging the soldiers for chewing gum (Wrigley's Spearmint), chocolate and oranges. The soldiers, exceptionally kind, had these items and gave them to us children. I have since come to learn that the US distributed Red Cross food parcels to each DP, including children, and I presume the US soldiers had access to items such as these as well. These parcels contained cube sugar, tins of cheddar cheese, Nescafe, corned beef, tuna, Spam, dried milk, Crisco, half pound chocolate bars, American cigarettes and sticks of gum. As I will recount later, the Red Cross boxes were dismantled by the UNRRA staff and individual items were distributed on a ration basis to each man, woman and child. Since children were counted as individuals, they received the rationed contents of the food packages as well, and the more children, the more food received, and the more items that could be used as barter. This practice of food distribution to civilians carried over into Manhattan in the 1950's where my family went to a military armory in midtown Manhattan to receive parcels of dried milk, cans of evaporated milk, lard and spam.

Some Additional Information about Displaced Persons Camps

Displaced Persons (DP's) were assembled and aggregated into camps according to nationality or religion. Their housing, in the case of the camps in which my family resided, were composed of multilevel buildings, with rooms assigned according to the size of their family. There were roughly 400 such camps in all of Germany.

I have read a first-hand account of the organization and administration of dealing with the DPs from the book, *The Wild Place (1953)*, by Katherine Hulme, an American volunteer working with the UNRRA, and the book, *Strangers in the Wild Place* (2013) by Adam Seipp, an Associate Professor of History at Texas A&M University. Hulme was an assistant UNRRA administrator assigned in 1945 to the camp at Wildflecken where tens of thousands of refugees were brought in by train, 40 boxcars at a time, 25 people to a car, from various parts of Germany. Seipp expands on Hulme's reminescences, and places into historical perspective the DP experiences. Wildflecken is the camp in which Elvis Presley was stationed when he was drafted in the 1950s into the army, but in the mid 1940s just after the war, it was the epicenter of the American effort to care for the DPs. During Hulme's administrative appointment, she was assigned to Schweinfurt and

Aschaffenburg and eventually was in charge of many camps over a broad region of Germany. Hulme is also the author of the well-known novel, *The Nun's Story*, which in 1952 was turned into a movie. She has an interesting biography including being a welder, a journalist, and a groupie of Gurdjieff. Hulme applied for work with the UNRRA and was assigned to work with the repatriation of the DPs. In her book, *The Wild Place*, she describes the operation of the overcrowded camps; securing food with help from the US army or local farmers, working with the US Third Army to keep an eye on the local German population as well as the expellees, the Germans that had been expelled from regions of Poland, Czechoslovakia, and Ukraine, and processing the DPs so that they could be repatriated to their former countries. Hulme describes that, as the DPs learned of the conditions in their former countries and the treatment that Stalin meted out to those that had fled west, they refused to be repatriated. This was also the story I heard from my Mom and Babcha in New York City when I was a child. No matter the incentives offered by the UNRRA, such as the offer of 14 days of food to be taken with them for the journey to their former country, the DP's, including my family refused to go back. Fourteen days of food does not sound like much in 2020, but at the end of the war this was considered a huge incentive. Therefore, the situation in the US zone of occupation was as follows: the region had a large US army presence with all the logistics of housing and feeding the troops, a large number of Displaced Persons i.e. non-Germans that were administered by the UNRRA, large numbers of German expellees who were expected to fend for themselves, and the local Germans who were the defeated enemy.

The DP camps were not what you may think, especially if all you've heard of is concentration camps. The pictures I have seen and stories I have read in Katherine Hulme's and Adam Seipp's books of refugees in the US sector, and descriptions I've seen and read on the internet, paint a picture of whole communities of individuals that had schools, barbershops, churches and newspapers, the whole gamut of social organization of civilian communities. These people do not appear emaciated or dressed in rags, at least not in the photos of the displaced persons' camps that I have seen on the internet, or the pictures of my family that I have in my possession. I assume that the pictures that I have seen, were of these peoples after they had recovered somewhat from the war. Katherine Hulme's book recounts how the camps were segregated by ethnic origin; either Poles, Latvians, Lithuanians, Ukrainians, or Jews. My family's birth documents showed Polish nationality so this is probably why we were assigned to Schweinfurt, which was exclusive to Poles. Very shortly thereafter, in 1947, we were assigned to the Aschaffenburg Camp which was populated by Ukrainians, Estonians and Byelorussians. Hume became the administrator of the Aschaffenburg camp, where my brother Dmytro was born, and so I imagine that my mother, with me or Dmytro in her arms, and Mary as a four-year old might have seen Hume walking about in the camp. Hulme was transferred to Wurtzburg in 1948 and took over a new area that stretched all the way to the Soviet zone in the east and to the Tyrol in the south, with about 65,000 DP's living in 73 scattered installations. As a part of her job she was also responsible for vocational training schools to prepare DP's for jobs that might take them to the US under the Displaced Person Act, which the Eightieth Congress passed on June 25, 1948. Her other duties included closing down the camps by 1950. Her book describes the difficulties she had feeding, housing and clothing the DP's, processing them for emigration, and for those going to the

US, eventually providing the transportation to Bremerhaven. Her description gave me an image of what life was like for my family in Germany. I include in this memoir a photo of my mom, Mary and Dmytro and I on a train to Bremerhaven in 1950. My father had died in Aschaffenburg in 1947, so I don't know who had taken this photo, and I am also not sure why my Babcha is not in the photo. As an aside, as I've already pointed out, in the eventual agreement on the zones of occupation, the US gained a seaport access around Bremen. Bremerhaven, the seaport of Bremen, contained immigration processing after Ellis Island was shut down, and was considered US territory.

The only direct information I have on the camps where my family lived, is through a few photos, and some official documents that I have in my possession. As an example, the photo shown in Figure 9 is of a room in the camp in Aschaffenburg during a Christmas dinner in 1947. Shown is my mother holding me in her arms and my father standing next to her, Babcha siting with Mary on her lap, and a table covered with dishes that apparently held food. There is another woman seated next to Babcha and Mary, one other woman with a child in arms, and a partial image of a man seated with a guitar. These other people are members of the other four families that shared the one room living quarters. Everyone appears finely dressed and looking forward into the camera.

Figure 9. Photo of a Christmas dinner in Aschaffenburg just after my first birthday in 1947.

This photo is consistent with the description given in Hulme's book. The food at the party was most likely from Red Cross packages or items that may have been bartered for the event. Other photos included below show me standing on a grassy patch of earth when I was about a year old, and of my mom and dad posing for the photo dressed in what appears to be gray clothing: my father in a gray suit and my mom in a gray skirt and white blouse. When I was a child, I was told by my mother that these clothes were sewn by her from army blankets, something that was not allowed per Hulme's account but overlooked by the administrators.

Figure 10. Photo of my mom and dad, taken in probably Aschaufenburg in 1947, in their 'horse blanket' clothing.

Figure 11. Photo of me in Germany, probably Aschaffenburg, at approximately one year old.

My dad died within six months of the date of this picture. He was 26 years old, and left a pregnant wife, two children (Mary and me), and his mother. My brother Dmytro was born one month after my father's death. Mary tells me that he had gone to the German dentist to take care of a toothache and for a few days and weeks afterward he complained of pain in his left arm and chest. After some time, he went to the camp hospital to have this checked out but because it was the feast of Pentecost, he could be seen only by a resident doctor as opposed to a Ukrainian doctor that would typically would be on call. The resident was unfamiliar with him and, gave him a sleeping pill at around 1pm. He was bedded down at the hospital. He woke up at about 11pm and, my sister tells me, his last words were, "doctor I'm dying". My mother and Babcha weren't informed of his death until the next day. I was also told by Mary that my mother and Babcha returned that evening to wash and clean the body for burial, a process that seems inconceivable in our current Western culture. I include below several photographs including a picture of my father in a coffin at the burial site, with me in my mother's arms, and another photo showing my Babcha standing next to the grave monument. Mary tells me that my dad's was an unusually large funeral with three priests in attendance.

Figure 12. Photo of my dad's funeral. Notice that at the right of the photo, Babcha is holding Mary and my mom is holding me.

Figure 13. Photo of Babcha standing at my Dad's monument in Aschaffenburg. Nick visited Germany sometime in the 90s and was not able to find the monument. Apparently, a housing project was built on top of this cemetery.

Processing for Emigration to the US

I've heard stories of my poor health in Germany, and Hulme and Seipp describe how the major factor in processing the DP's out of the camps was health and communicable diseases. I have read that tuberculosis was rampant in Europe after the war and, in fact, Babcha and I both tested positive for the TB virus. The countries of emigration had strict rules against allowing sick or enfeebled people, or those believed to be a security risk, to emigrate. Hulme describes sad cases where DPs committed suicide when they came to know that they had tuberculosis, or some other communicable disease, and therefore would not be accepted into the US. I've been told that I had severe sore throats and that I was nursed back to health by Babcha. I was also told that when my family was being processed to leave Germany and was undergoing medical exams, my mother sheparded me through the health inspection, trying to somehow disguise my illness so that we wouldn't be turned back. Babcha had a difficult time getting clearance to leave for the US, because she had a 'stain' in her lungs and after another x-ray she was able to catch up with us.

Figure 14. Photo of my mom, Mary, me and Dmytro in a train window on our way to Bremerhaven, most likely in December 1950. We were finally on our way to the US. My Babcha is not in the photo most likely because she had to undergo additional medical tests.

Hulme says in her book that it was especially difficult for 'single women or women with children without noticeable means of support' to emigrate to the US. Most countries adjusted their immigration policies to insist that immigrants contribute to the economic welfare of the country and/or have sponsorship by a citizen of the country, and this was especially so for the US. For example, the Displaced Persons Act of 1948 and the Amendment to the Act of 1950 stipulated that "…assurance would be given by a citizen or citizens of the US and that the immigrant will be suitably employed without displacing some other person from employment and…shall not become public charges and will have housing without displacing some other person". The Amendment to the Act also stipulated that orphans could, *in lieu of affidavits*, could be provided such assurance by a US citizen or organization. This language was provided for the benefit of Jews that had been liberated from concentration camps, and especially young children who had lost one or both parents.

My family's future was very precarious, especially in 1947, because of the death of my father, and of the short list of countries to which we might emigrate. Initially, the camps were due to be shut down by 1950, so there was little time to complete the processing for immigration to the US.

By the way, when I was a child, I recall hearing from my mother that she had a choice of emigrating to Argentina, Rhodesia (currently Zimbabwe), Canada or the US, and that everyone wanted to emigrate to the US, whose streets were 'paved with gold.' This is a story that has been widely repeated by many DPs and which you can read about on the internet. I have met several distant cousins who had emigrated to Argentina so there were decisions made that placed DPs all over the world. Who knows what my life would have been like had my mom made a different decision.

More on Emigration processing

Emigration to the US was an especially politicized problem during and after the war-there was a sentiment of anti-immigration in the US-and there was debate as to limiting the amount of people and a time frame within which the immigrants were to be allowed into the country. However, as I've stated above, Congress, with the support of President Truman, passed the Displaced Persons Act of 1948, and the Amendment of this act in 1950. The Act initially allowed for the immigration of about 200,000 DP's, forty percent of whom had to be from 'territories annexed by a foreign power' and thirty percent had to be farmers. My family as well as the other families in the DP camp fell under this deadline so there was much anxiety to complete the processing documents and leave Germany by 1950. Katherine Hulme writes about the anxiety by her staff to rush to complete the processing by 1950, and to close the camps. As the deadline for extension for the Act neared, my family faced the possibility of being left behind 'as foreigners' in Germany. I have read that Truman administration officials argued that the US needed to help the Jews who had been in concentration camps and to modify the Immigration Law to include orphans and, extend the time limit to 1952. The Amendment stipulated that eventually about 410,000 individuals, some 200,000 more than sited in the Immigration Act of 1948, would also include orphans for permanent residency. Given the approach of the 1950 deadline, and the death of my father, my family was slated to be one of the last to leave in 1950. I am not sure if we were admitted to the US under the 1948 Act of Congress or its Amendment. As an aside, the Amendment specifies that 4,000 immigrants living in China as a result of the war, to be admitted to the US. This fact became important to me since I would come to meet and know one of these immigrants, who I worked for just after Dorothea and I got married. I'll say more about her later.

My family had little of value when they left their village, and I imagine they did not earn hard currency working for the Germans, so that when they eventually ended up in the DP camp in Schweinfurt, they did not have the resources or the ability to purchase foodstuffs or articles of clothing. This changed after the takeover of the camps by UNRRA and the distribution of the Red Cross food allotment. You can appreciate that if a person had cigarettes, these could be sold on the 'black market' or traded for other personal items. This type of commerce could then be used to also purchase services from people such as barbers, seamstresses, and lawyers. In addition to documentation, the emigration to the US required a US sponsor who would provide financial assurance for the immigrants, and there were many organizations and individuals in the US that would do this. In my family's case, a Ukrainian lawyer in Aschaffenburg, John Kunitsky, who had relatives in New York, befriended my mother and father and promised to help in the arrangements to sponsor my family. He left for the US prior to us and worked out the arrangements for his brother's family, through the Catholic church in Manhattan, to sponsor us. Once my mom obtained the sponsorship of the Kunitskys, our processing continued.

Sponsorship of the Kunitsky Family

It is astounding to me, even now, to think that someone in the US would commit to sponsor an unknown family for immigration. This is what Mr. and Mrs. Kunitsky did for me and my family. Without this commitment from them, I wouldn't be where I am, and I am overwhelmed each time I think of this. As I've said above, the Displaced Persons Act stipulated that applicants must present guarantees by US sponsors that housing was waiting and that they wouldn't displace American workers from jobs. The sponsors also needed to provide assurances that the immigrants would not become public charges. We would come to depend on the Kunitsky family to provide these assurances.

My knowledge of the Kunitsky family comes from my sister Mary, and Mary Kuniky (having simplified her name from Kunitsky), who was married to Nick (later changing his name to Neal). The patriarch of the family, 'Pan' Kunitsky, had emigrated to the US early in the 20th century (I believe in 1900) to Pittsburgh. He worked in the coal industry and eventually moved to NYC where he met and married 'Pani' Kunitsky. Mr. (William) and Mrs. Kunitsky were called Pan and Pani, an honorific meaning sir and madam in Polish and Ukrainian. I enclose a photo of Pani

Kunitsky, she was known as Babi by her grandchildren, in about 1960 as well as the wedding picture of Neal and his wife Mary. The Kunitskys lived near and attended St. George Church and, while I was a boy, I visited them at their apartment on 15th Street in Manhattan, and saw them at church. They had four children, the youngest being in their early 20's; Neal (married to Mary Pretiatko), Jerry (married to Elaine, whose maiden name I do not know), Anne (married to Pete Switnicky) and Katherine (Kashi who was married but I do not know her husband's name). They lived on 15th Street between 1st and 2nd Avenue, eight blocks from the church. I recall Nick and Jerry as young men who took me and Dmytro under their wing. They bought us toys and goodies to eat and took us for rides in their 1956 Buick Roadmaster convertible. To give you one example of their kindness I'll relate a story that has stayed with me all my life: one day Nick took Dmytro and I for a ride in the neighborhood and we stopped at a toy/candy store on Avenue A. He took us inside and then said that I should pick out anything I wanted and he would buy it for me. In spite of my being about 10 years old, I became anxious and modified my request to some small toy truck in spite of what I really wanted, which I realized would have been too big a request. I remember other instances of rides in Nick's car, and it never ceases to amaze me that a 20-something young man would take immigrant children for rides in his car.

The Kunitskys were also the ones that took care to get a place for us to live, and I assume provided the first of the food we had to eat and drink. They got us our first apartment and, as was the 'custom' of the time, they paid $300 to the superintendent of the building "to get us the keys to our apartment". You may know that apartments in NYC are rent-controlled, meaning that the rent you agree to pay will remain fixed for the duration of your rental, except for small increases to account for inflation, or improvements made by the landlord. So, the system was as follows: when a tenant moves out, the superintendent is the first to know about it, and it had become common practice for the 'super' to provide this information to select tenants or friends, for a fee. The practice of giving money to the 'super' is of course corruption, but this is how the system worked. You handed over money to the super for the key to the apartment, then you signed a lease and moved in. The Kunitsky's paid this fee for us. Besides the one-time fee of $300, the rent as I recall was $25/month.

Figure 15. A wedding photograph of Mary and Neal Kunicky (Nick Kunitsky was the name by which I had known him). I reconnected with Mary and her family in 2016 when she was living in the suburbs of Hartford, Connecticut. Neal developed Alzheimer's and was confined to a nursing home for about five years (2012-2017), and died in 2017 at the age of 87.

Figure 16. Photo of Pani Kunitsky taken in Fox Chase, PA, c.1960.

We crossed the Atlantic in December 1950, headed for New York, on the S.S. General George C. Muir, a troop ship that was converted to a civilian transport. I was nearly five years old. My Babcha was not with us because she had failed the final medical inspection at the time the family was being processed for boarding. This delay put her on another ship, the General Stewart and she arrived in NYC one month later. I do not know by what means my Babcha lived in Bremerhaven while she waited to get a new medical inspection. I was told by Mary that Babcha's sponsor was Anne Kunitsky. She was engaged to be married and she paid $500 for Babcha's sponsorship, a huge amount of money by 1950s standards. I am not sure who received this payment. I include two documents: one from the St. George Church and the other a deposition of Anna Kunitsky, to the IRO (International Relief Organization) Resettlement Center regarding sponsorship of my Babcha to show an example of the type of legal documents were required to immigrate to the US.

An Improbable Circumstance

I will relate one out-of-time sequence story pertaining to my being in a DP camp in Aschaffenburg. After Dorothea and I were married, we lived on East 53rd Street and Avenue N in Brooklyn, just three blocks from Dorothea's parents, and as you would expect we would frequently attend family gatherings at holidays and met the Rumstich relations at some of these affairs. At one such time in 1966, just after Christine was born, we were visited by Uncle Mac (Ernest Vernon MacClellan) and Tante (Aunt) Hildegarde. Tante Hildegarde was not a relation by blood but had a close connection with Dorothea's parents and was considered a part of the family, ergo Dorothea calling her Tante. Hildegarde Gogge was born in Kiel in 1915, to the best friend of Dorothea's paternal grandmother. Hildegarde and her mother emigrated to the US sometime in the 20s and were awaiting the father/husband to arrive on a later boat. During this wait, Hildegarde's mother died. Hildegarde was 8 years old at this time, and Nanni and Wilhelm (Dorothea's fraternal grandmother and grandfather) took Hildegrade into their household and raised her as a daughter. I'm not sure why the father dropped out of the picture at this time. In any event, when she grew up, Tante Hildegarde married Uncle Mac, a WWI and WWII veteran, and they lived on a farm in Gettysburg, PA. Uncle Mac had risen to the rank of Lt. Colonel before discharge from the US Army. Now getting back to the visit of Tante Hildegarde and Uncle Mac to our little apartment. During the course of our conversation I mentioned that I was an immigrant being born in Schweinfurt and lived in Aschaffenburg just after the war. Uncle Mac began to tell me that as a Lt. Colonel in the US military after WWII, he was an adjutant for several camps in Germany, including Aschaffenburg, during the time that I was there in 1947. An adjutant is the senior officer in charge of supplies and provisions. This was the only time that I recall seeing him and talking to him about his work as a US Army Lt. Colonel in Germany. He died in 1972 in Adams, PA and Tante Hildgarde died in 1994. It seems incredible that he was providing the food and clothing for the camp while I was there and that our paths may have crossed.

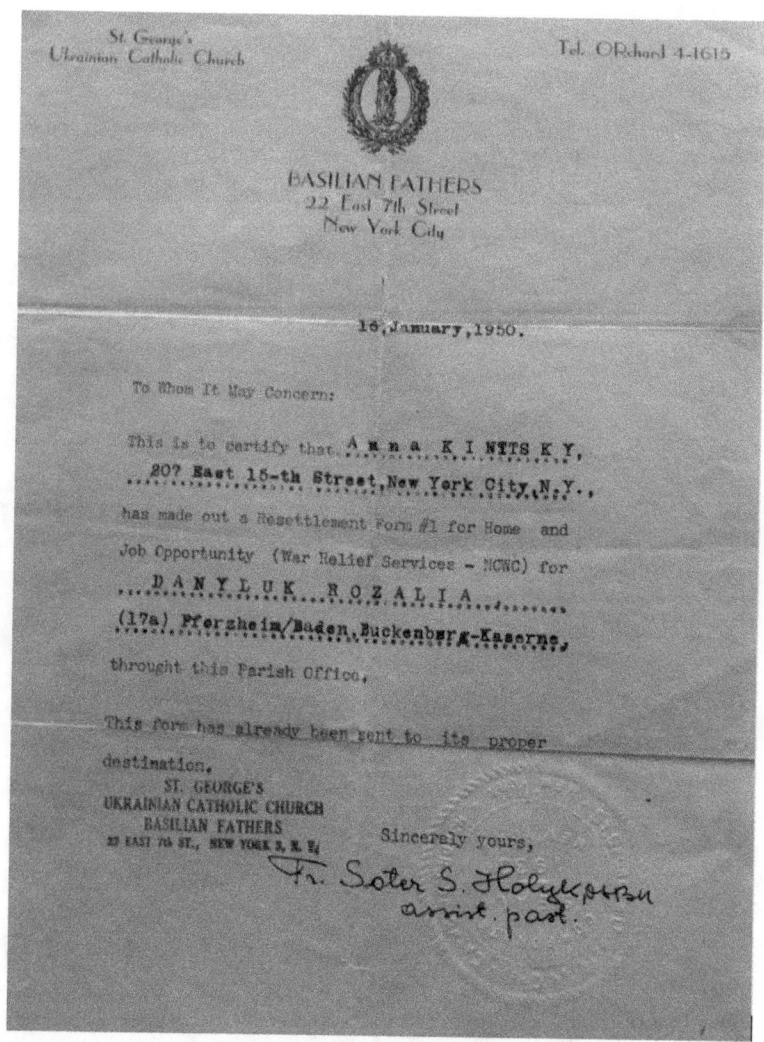

Figure 17. Resettlement document certifying the commitment made by Anna Kunitsky.

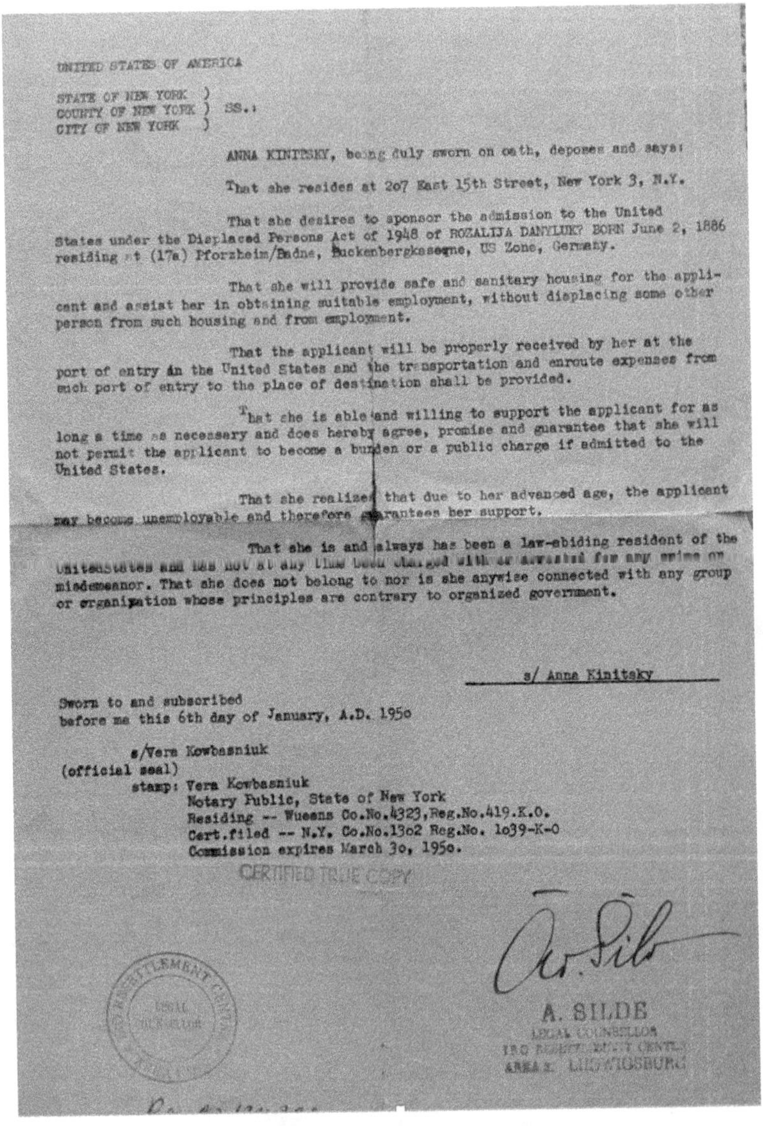

UNITED STATES OF AMERICA

STATE OF NEW YORK)
COUNTY OF NEW YORK) SS.:
CITY OF NEW YORK)

ANNA KINITSKY, being duly sworn on oath, deposes and says:

That she resides at 207 East 15th Street, New York 3, N.Y.

That she desires to sponsor the admission to the United States under the Displaced Persons Act of 1948 of ROZALIJA DANYLUK? BORN June 2, 1886 residing at (17a) Pforzheim/Badne, Buckenbergkasegne, US Zone, Germany.

That she will provide safe and sanitary housing for the applicant and assist her in obtaining suitable employment, without displacing some other person from such housing and from employment.

That the applicant will be properly received by her at the port of entry in the United States and the transportation and enroute expenses from such port of entry to the place of destination shall be provided.

That she is able and willing to support the applicant for as long a time as necessary and does hereby agree, promise and guarantee that she will not permit the applicant to become a burden or a public charge if admitted to the United States.

That she realizes that due to her advanced age, the applicant may become unemployable and therefore guarantees her support.

That she is and always has been a law-abiding resident of the UnitedStates and has not at any time been charged with or arrested for any crime or misdemeanor. That she does not belong to nor is she anywise connected with any group or organization whose principles are contrary to organized government.

s/ Anna Kinitsky

Sworn to and subscribed
before me this 6th day of January, A.D. 1950

s/Vera Kowbasniuk
(official seal)
stamp: Vera Kowbasniuk
Notary Public, State of New York
Residing -- Wueens Co.No.4323,Reg.No.419.K.O.
Cert.filed -- N.Y. Co.No.1302 Reg.No. 1039-K-0
Commission expires March 30, 1950.

CERTIFIED TRUE COPY

A. SILDE
LEGAL COUNSELLOR

Figure 18. Photograph of a legal document.

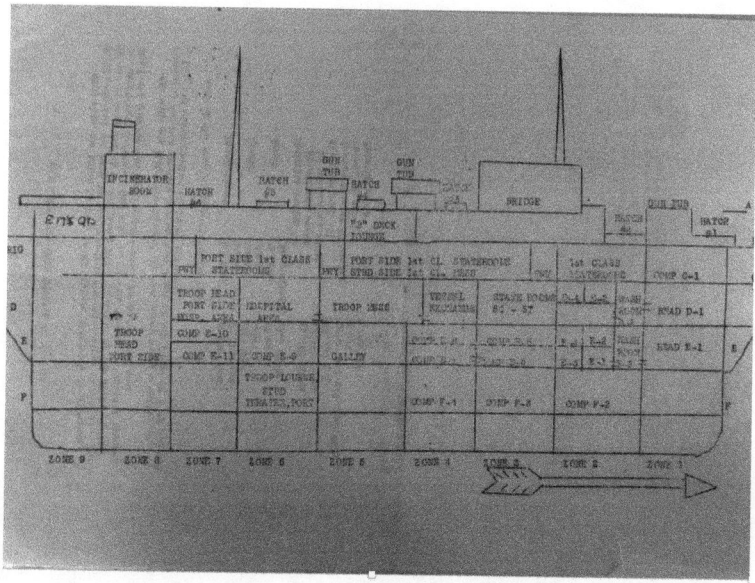

Figure 19. Schematic diagram of the General Muir,
obtained from the Student Tour Group report.

Figure 20. Photograph of the General C.H. Muir, a troop transport converted
after WWII to carry displaced persons from Europe to the US.

Crossing Over

We departed for the US on the USS General C.H. Muir (Figure 18). This ship, designated as T-AP-142, a troop transport, was launched in Nov. 24, 1944 in Richmond, California. It was acquired by the US Navy, decommissioned and then returned to the Maritime Commission and eventually turned over to the Army Transportation Services on 18 June 1946. Besides her other commissions, the ship transported DP's to the US between 1946 and 1950. This ship typically accommodated 228 officers and 3,595 enlisted men, but I do not know how many DP's were crammed into the ship during a typical trip. I have read in the book by Roman Mac (listed in the references) who also came over to the US on the General Muir, that the DPs walked on to the ship by way of a gangplank where an administrator checked each DP's documents and medical certifications. Besides photos of the ship, I have also found a Student Sea Tour Souvenir Document dated 4 August-9 September 1950, on their return voyage to the US, which shows a cross section of the schematic of the ship (Fig. 17); location of the Mess Hall, sleeping quarters, the head (toilet), theater and other parts, and a description of the ship activities such as church services, lectures, choral groups activities, movies, and dancing. The Student Sea Tour Group was composed of college students that made pilgrimages to areas of the US, but others went to Europe, as part of a cultural exchange and learning program. The Tour Group Report that I have in my possession mentions an evening where different ethnic groups exchanged songs, and that prior to the return voyage, the Captain called representatives of the ethnic groups together and informed them of the rules of behavior, and organization of the entertainment committee. I found it interesting that one of the movies mentioned in the Student Sea Tour Document was 'The Third Man", a movie directed by Orson Welles and which I have seen many times. The ship also functioned as a DP transport for about 1 and a half years. Using the number of troops as a typical number, the General Muir carried about 20,000 people to the US during the time of its service as a DP transport. I have no memory of the social and cultural activities mentioned in the Tour Group report, but I doubt that these activities would have been going on in the transport of DPs.

I found another interesting reference to the General Muir in a book by Boak who worked for the Office of Special Services (OSS), the precursor of the Central Intelligence Agency, in the Pacific theatre of the war, and where he describes sailing to Malaysia and Burma on the General Muir in January 1945. I will quote his description since it is so interesting and amusing:

The ship has seven decks and "well below the waterline latrine (the 'head' in shipboard terminology) consists of the usual through-like urinals lined up against a bulkhead, and long line of lidless commodes that were, it turned out, connected more or less directly to the ocean. Certain Pacific swells would occasionally resonate throughout this disposal system and transform those commodes into gigantic bidets. Those unfortunate enough to be perched there at the time found themselves shockingly atop a salty geyser".

My mother, two siblings and I sailed out of Bremerhaven, in

the bowels of the ship, which I recall had sleeping bunks in dark rooms, with light bulbs enclosed in metal cages on the ceiling. By the 'bowel of the ship' I mean the region below the water line, without a port hole, in the center of the ship, that had bunks meant for soldiers. Dmytro was about three at the time and likely not allowed far from our mother but I remember climbing in and out of an upper bunk to roam the ship, and my mom being seasick throughout most of the journey. The stench of vomit was everywhere and kept the passengers sick throughout the voyage. I was not seasick and recall being asked by my mother to get her an apple or orange since she couldn't keep anything else down, and after running around the ship I finally found an apple, for which my mom was grateful. If you read the DP Act of 1948 you will see that the US government also provided financial assistance for the passage and incidentals, by which I take it to mean food, through the Reconstruction Finance Corporation. This was a civilian corporation that was provided money by the US government, with deferred interest on the repayment of the loan, to support the transport of the DPs. I have seen photos of other passengers on this ship, with men in suits and ties and women smartly dressed, so I assume that there were various types of passengers on board, the well off and the poor. The cross section of the ship lists staterooms which means to me that there was a variety of social classes on board. You may find it interesting that there is a delicatessen restaurant in Atlanta, called the General Muir, partly owned by a woman whose grandparents and great grandparents also travelled to the US on the General Muir sometime prior to my family's voyage. She named her restaurant the General Muir in honor of her grandparents. Dorothea and I met this woman and she told us that her great grandparents were Polish Jews who were trapped in an internment camp during the war where her great grandfather was a doctor in charge of providing medical care for the camp. She had heard stories of the trip from her grandparents, and I saw pictures of them on the walls of the restaurant. She also told us that there has been some organization of periodic reunion of the DPs that were transported on the General Muir but I haven't followed up on this.

On the morning that the ship entered New York harbor, December 13, 1950, after a 12-day voyage, I recall the buildup of excitement, chatter and clambering of the passenger's topside. I didn't know what this was about but I came to know later that the passengers expected to see the Statue of Liberty. Unfortunately, I missed the event and did not see the majestic statue as we entered New York harbor. I have in my possession a copy of the Declaration of Intention signed by my mother and the place of foreign residence listed as Phortsheim, the emigration point Bremerhaven, and the date Dec. 13, 1950, arriving on the C.H. General Muir. I assume we were issued 'green cards' in Bremerhaven prior to boarding but I don't have information or documents to confirm this.

Mary has told me how she remembers disembarking near Times Square, and waiting at the dock for several hours before someone, I do not know who, picked us up. The schematic diagram from the Student Tour Group (Fig. 21) shows the path of the General Muir through New York Harbor, with a landing at Times Square, i.e. at 42nd Street and the Hudson River. I now imagine my family, a young woman with three kids sitting on a bench, their meager belongings in a suitcase, watching other passengers being met by family or friends, and the crowd dispersing until there was no one left except for us, and perhaps one or two other stragglers.

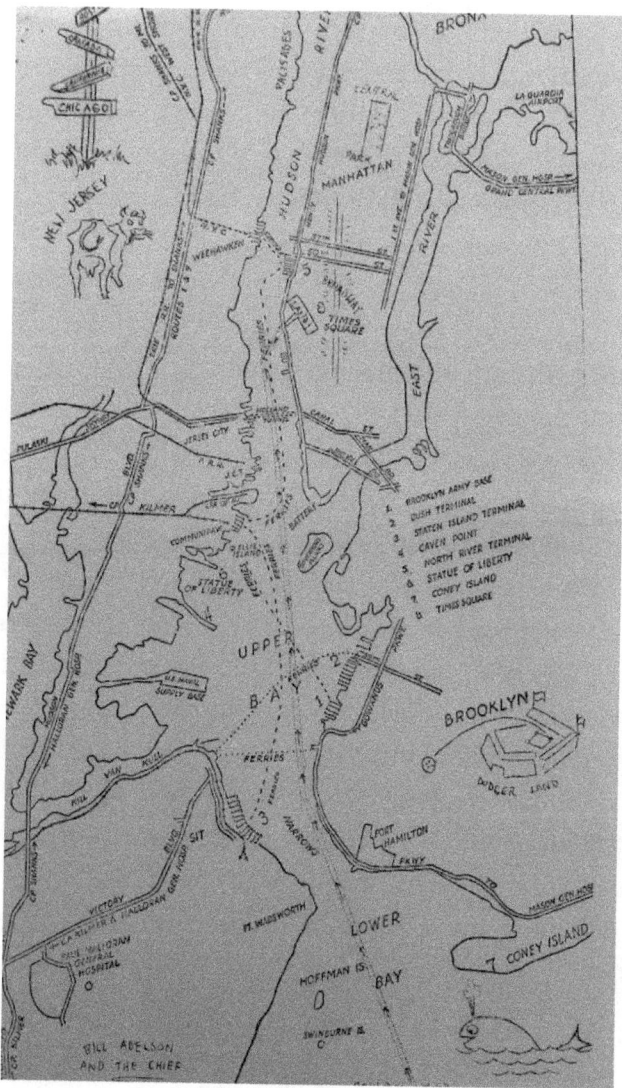

Figure 21. Schematic of New York Harbor and the path of the General Muir on its way toward Times Square as shown in the Student Tour Group document. If you follow the dashed line coming into New York Harbor, past Brooklyn, you will see that the ship stopped at Times Square on the Hudson River.

The map in the Student Tour Report shows that the ship, on that September crossing, landed near Times Square and Mary tells me that the location of our disembarkation was the same in December. We departed Bremerhaven on December 2 and arrived in NYC on December 13. I have tried to find some news of our trip in the NY Times and New York Herald Tribune looking for the arrival records of a ship full of DPs but apparently, this docking was no longer very interesting news to New Yorkers. Eventually we met up with Katherine Kunitsky who took us to a friend, who had an apartment on 81st Street on the east side of Manhattan where we stayed for about four weeks. It is also mind-boggling to imagine a single woman taking in a (foreign) family to live with her for a month. After those first few weeks we shared an apartment with another young couple on Avenue A, between 13th and 14th streets, and later moved to the more permanent apartment on 7th Street. The apartment on Avenue A was a railroad flat design and I have vivid memories of looking out the front window, and the sound of singing of our canary which my mother bought. As I said earlier, I don't know who paid the rent for the apartment on 7th Street, how the groceries or clothes were purchased, but I presume it was the Kunitskys who took care of this. I will describe various details of this apartment on 7th Street a little later in this memoir.

Figure 22. Photo of the street-side of the tenement of the 7th Street address we lived in. The building, built in 1920, is a six-story structure with a five-step stoop. We lived on the third floor facing the back. The rent of a single unit in the 1950's was $25/month but in today's market, 2019, goes for about $4,000/month (see the realty agency Streeteasy for photos of the renovated insides).

Part 2

New York in the 1950's

New York of the 1950's just after WWII was one of the primary ports of entry for immigrants to the US. It was exciting to arrive in this big city, and as one example of how different it was from any experience an immigrant would have, I'll mention my mothers' description, which she told me many years later. She said that she had never seen as many lights at one place, and that these lights turned the night into day. She also said that she found it hard to believe that the stores had fruit for sale, and especially strawberries in the middle of the winter. The area of Manhattan where we settled seemed to be all about noise, lights, exhaust from automobiles and the screech of overhead, elevated trains. I have vivid memories of this noise, demolition of old housing and the construction of public housing, wood fires in open black 'oil' drums on street corners in the winter, pushcarts on Delancy and Orchard Streets and watching TV in storefront windows. Millions of New Yorkers especially the immigrants lived in ethnic ghettos, and the Lower East Side especially, was divided into neighborhoods with ethnic groups sponsoring new immigrants. The area around 7th Street and the Bowery near St. George Church was where the Catholic Ukrainians came to be settled, and this is the area that I think of as the Ukrainian ghetto. To give you some idea as to the numbers of Ukrainians living in our 'ghetto' I estimate a number such as 10,000 individuals (60 buildings per block, 20 apartments per tenement, 4 persons in each family, 28 blocks with ¼ being Ukrainians). I include a photo of the still-standing tenement on 7th Street in which we lived and it shows that our building is six stories tall, one story taller than the typical others. These types of tenements stood shoulder-to-shoulder along the streets and avenues of the Lower East Side of Manhattan, some of the buildings separated from their neighbors by an alleyway five or six feet wide. Besides the tenements there also were Brownstone houses, three of four story tall buildings, rows of which started on 10th Street west of Second Avenue, that were built by wealthy New Yorkers during the heydays of the 19th century. This is another case of my local environment being worlds away from that lived by the local 'American' population. It was exciting to be a kid roaming about in the big city, and I recall digging through huge piles of bricks, waiting to be recycled, from the demolition of tenements near Houston Street, looking for perceived 'treasure,' such as lost jewelry, watches or other artifacts. By 1950 the previous generation of immigrants, those that arrived at the turn of the 20th century before WWI and in between the two world wars, or lucky enough to have escaped the war, were assimilating and moving to the upper east and west sides of Manhattan, into New Jersey, Brooklyn and The Bronx, and the newly-arrived were moving into the vacated tenements.

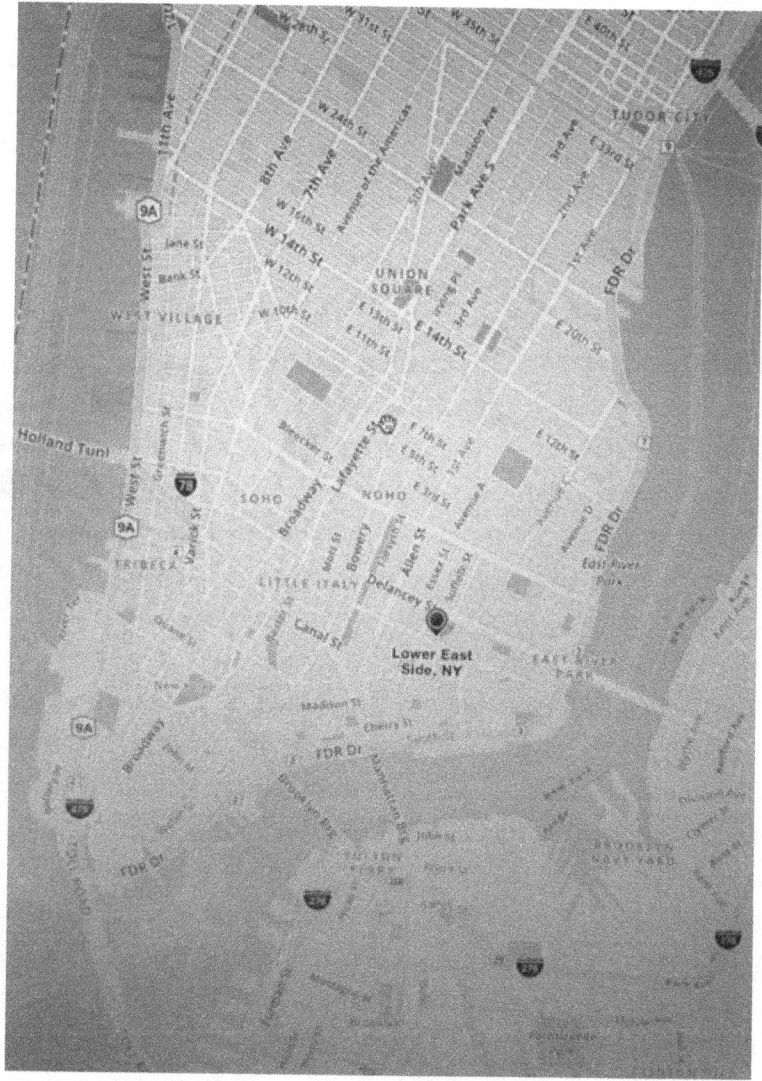

Figure 23. Modern era map of the lower east side of Manhattan showing the area where I grew up, around 7th Street and First Avenue.

I include a map of Manhattan, Figure 23, to show you the neighborhood of Manhattan which contained the Ukrainian community and in which we lived. The area occupied by the Ukrainians was fairly small, roughly encompassing the region between 1st and 14th Streets and Avenue A and the Bowery. The Ukrainians were anchored by St. George Catholic Church located on 7th street between 2nd Avenue and the Bowery, more precisely on the corner of Taras Shevchenko and Seventh Streets. We were surrounded by the Jews, Italians, Poles, Puerto Ricans, Chinese, and Beatniks, and each of these ethnic groups had their houses of worship, except for the Beatniks, of course. For example, there was a Polish church on 7th Street between Avenue A and 1st Avenue, an Orthodox Ukrainian Church on 15th Street, a Synagogue on 6th Street near Avenue C, a Russian Orthodox church on 10th Street and Avenue A, and a National Polish Catholic Church on St. Mark's Place (8th Street) between 1st and 2nd Avenue. A house of worship on almost every block. There was public housing which bordered the East River at Houston Street. The neighborhood also contained Cooper Union, Stuyvesant Town, and New York University to name just a few of these still-existing older organizations, and of course there were many other native New Yorkers living among us. Growing up in lower Manhattan near the coal-fired Power (Consolidated Edison) Plant on 14th Street and the East River, boys would jump into the river on hot summer days to cool off even though this was the location of the overflow sewage discharge. The jump would be timed between discharges or postponed for the days when the discharge did not occur. There was also a public swimming pool at 23rd Street where you could swim for a 10 cents entry fee, Bellevue Hospital on 27th Street, and the United Nations Building on 42nd Street. The UN building was a marvel to me, modern looking and unlike anything in the city. By the way, I have read a story in the Wall Street Journal on Sept. 19, 2019 that the city is looking into building a swimming pool, sitting in the East River, near the location of the pool which I have mentioned. The article stated that the major issue was designing a filtering system because of this discharge, which is apparently still going on. Today, I would not go into this pool no matter how efficient the filtration system.

When I was about 10 years old, Dmytro and I would walk to Central Park and on one or two occasions, made our way to the Museum of Natural History and the Planetarium on the west side of 82nd Street, about 4 miles from our apartment. It is easy to calculate distances in Manhattan since the north/south block length, the short dimension of the rectangle, was 21 blocks to the mile. This was my world and with the exception of the places like Central Park and the swimming pool and the other places I've mentioned above, we generally stayed in our neighborhood.

In the 1950's, St. George's Church was the focus of the Ukrainian community and as I've said, it was located at 7th Street, just east of the Bowery, and adjacent to one of the buildings of Cooper Union. The old church building was demolished sometime in the late 1960's and a new church built at the same spot between the Bowery (which turns into 4th Avenue north of 9th Street) and a one-block street on the east side of the Cooper Union Building which has since been re-named Taras Shevchenko Street, after a famous Ukrainian writer and poet who lived in the 19th century. The Cooper Union is a private undergraduate and graduate school that is known for engineering and has a long history in New York City. This was the place where Abraham Lincoln delivered, in February 1860, his famous speech regarding his opposition to the expansion of slavery into the Missouri territory and propelled him to the presidency later that year. The building that housed St. George Church had been a Baptist church in the 1920's, was acquired by the Ukrainian community, and the street now called Taras Shevchenko did not have this name while I lived there. Cooper Union, which I associated with the building, bordering on Taras Shevchenko Street, looked formidable; the façade was made of large taupe-gray stones, with windows covered so that you could not see inside, and only one entrance on the 4th Avenue side. Where Taras Shevchenko Street intersects, and does not go beyond 7th Street, stands a NYC landmark, McSorley's Old Ale House, established in 1854, which is at the ground level of one of the tenements. McSorley's has been frequented by New Yorkers of all stripes but surprisingly it was not a place that the Ukrainians went to drink or congregate, although when I was a teenager I had been there to drink several mugs of ale. McSorley's served ale at 25 cents for two mugs and a plate of saltine crackers topped with raw onion rings (this cost $1.25). The neighborhood also contained expressly Ukrainian organizations such as the Ukrainian National Home, a quasi-political organization representing the political views of the community, Plast (the A sounds like the a in Art), the national headquarters of the boy scouts, Ecco, a Ukrainian potpourri store located next to McSorley's, and Orchidia, a bar on 9th Street and Second Avenue. Peter Jarema's, the funeral home on 7th street near Avenue A, was also Ukrainian. I mention these establishments because these were Ukrainian-only, run by Ukrainian merchants who knew practically all the Ukrainians living in the area. Besides the several greasy spoon restaurants in our area, the only restaurant I was familiar with was located inside the Ukrainian National Home, although I don't ever remember going to any restaurant. Although we didn't eat at restaurants, we would sometimes, get a hot dog from a local push cart vendor, the hot dog kept warmed in a steel tub of hot water, plopped on a soft hot dog bun, topped with mustard, cooked onions and relish and sauerkraut. Knishes were also sold by street vendors from a hand-pushed cart. There is nothing better than a knish sliced in half and slathered with mustard. In the summer, we got an 'ices' from a street vendor, a paper cup of 'shaved ice' scraped from a block of ice, sprinkled with drops of lemon or raspberry syrup from a water bottle with a spouted top, and chocolate covered ice cream bars, and creamsicles.

Figure 24. Photo of our family taken on 1st Avenue in about 1959. This photo shows Wasyl Bodnar and Nick and John at 3 and 4 years old.

Some Historical Details of the Neighborhood

Tenements in Manhattan are typically five story structures with a basement level residence, below street level, and a stoop-a stairway of about five to 10 steps leading to a front door-as seen in the photo I've included. The basement level sometimes had stairs leading down into an apartment or a retail business such as a grocery store. The front and back of the building contained a fire escape, metal structures with a ladder that led to the street. In the early 1950's the east-west section of Manhattan was bisected at 3rd Avenue by an elevated train track that ran from the South Ferry to Harlem, and such rail transportation lines in New York, which started out being private ventures, were turned into public utilities, and eventually became subways. When we arrived in Manhattan, the 3rd Avenue 'El' (the Interborough Transit System, or IRT) was an elevated train line that created lots of noise, dust and activity, since there was a stop at the Bowery at 8th Street, and the trains stopped and accelerated coming into and out of the station. I still, in my minds' eye, recall dust particles of brake debris, glittering from the sun reflecting from the particles, as they fell from the tracks, and it seemed as if everything was coated with it. I recall that sometime in the 50's this elevated line was dismantled and an underground subway put in place with a stop at the Bowery and Astor Place (around 8th Street and the location where the Bowery merges with Fourth Avenue or Park Avenue South as it was called in our area). The tenements and other buildings bounding the train tracks in this area of Manhattan housed the newly arrived and poor. This area near the corner of 2nd Avenue and 7th Street also had a vaudeville theatre, and I recall several occasions when the manager of the theatre would walk up and down the street handing out free tickets to fill the theatre, if it was sparsely filled with paying customers. We were given tickets even though the shows were sometimes risqué, having a strip tease act. I recall one such show with a strip tease act performed by what I perceived as an older woman, a male singer and a trained dog act. The strip tease act, to me, was not titillating, but perhaps I was too young to appreciate it. The streets were always filled with people. There were also many times when we, as teenage boys, were handed especially-packaged cigarettes, four to a small pack, as a way to introduce us kids to smoking. The 1950's represented the end of the vaudeville era, and as the 50's rolled on, the vaudeville theatres transformed into movie houses and off- and off off-Broadway theatres. You could find lots of unsavory characters (at least in the location of 7th Street); drunks and homeless men and women, and prostitutes. Walking to school in the morning you'd see derelicts, their pants flies open, sleeping on the sidewalk or in the alcoves of tenements. Whenever I ride the train in Chicago from downtown to the airport I'm reminded of the feeling of the Astor Place area with residential buildings so close to the elevated tracks that you could almost touch the window ledges from the train. The Bowery, especially south of Eight Street, had this reputation of homeless individuals and drunks.

In addition to the unsavory characters, you would occasionally see evangelists standing on 'soap boxes,' literally milk crates or other boxes, that elevated them above the listeners, so that they could be seen, bibles lifted into the air, admonishing passersby that they needed to repent in order to be saved. Sometimes a small crowd would gather, and listen or heckle. This region of Manhattan over most of the 20th century was also the site of many political demonstrations, especially at Union Square on 14th Street and Fourth Avenue. I've seen pictures of the 30's and 40's with large crowds listening to speakers talk about joining unions and demonstrations for the Communist Party. I don't recall any Union and Communist gatherings, and given their history, the Ukrainians stayed away. Sometime in the 60's, Union Square Park became surrounded with department stores such as Macy's, SKlein, and Lord and Taylor and this became a shopping destination from an area larger than our little neighborhood.

The Bowery also contained factory buildings such as the Steinway piano factory on Bowery and 8th Street and, used book stores. There were 14 used bookstores on 4th Avenue between Union Square and Astor Place and, I have come to know that this area was called Book Row, although this is not what I recall it being called. As I advanced in grade school, I liked to go to these bookstores to thumb through dusty old books, especially mathematics texts. I don't know why I was interested in mathematics texts but I recall wondering at the meaning of the 'integration' symbols and I promised myself that I would find out. Even at this early age I realized that one needed to know a lot of background to be able to read these texts. I still like old books and to this day, I like cracking open an old book, and thumbing through it; seeing if a previous reader has made any annotations, and feeling the paper with my fingers. I badgered my mother to buy us/me the Encyclopedia Britannica and at one time dragged her to one of these bookstores, but she said she could not afford to buy the books. She eventually did buy a one-volume book, the Columbia Encyclopedia, which I still have in my possession.

The Ukrainian neighborhood was adjacent to the Polish section around Avenue A and a small spill-over community of Italians who occupied the blocks between 10th street and First Avenue and 14th Street. The Italian men had, what I considered at the time, strange customs, such as eating raw shellfish and hanging out at the barbershop where they got haircuts, a shave and their shoes polished. It was an unspoken rule that you didn't interact with these groups.

Manhattan also has a large Chinese community south of Houston Street and west of 1st Avenue. It is still surprising to me that I had never ventured to Chinatown while I lived there. Chinatown was like a foreign country to me. The Chinese were another ethnic community that stuck together, spoke Chinese among themselves, and lived in their own ghetto. When I did venture out, my friends and I went into the Italian neighborhood, adjacent to the Chinese, during festivals or religious feasts, such as the Feast of San Gennaro.

Just south of 1st Street was a collection of streets, Delancy and Orchard Streets for example, crowded with pushcarts that stood shoulder-to-shoulder, wheeled into position each morning, forming a kind of bazaar with all kinds of goods for sale, from clothes and shoes to food. The business establishments, as well as the pushcarts on Delancy and Orchard streets, were run by Jewish merchants, some of whom also rented and ran a business from a storefront of a tenement next to where they positioned the pushcart. They sold dry goods and food, and one could buy a shirt, pants or shoes and smell whiffs of hot knishes, herring, pickles in great big barrels, and vegetables and fruit. I have read that in 1938, Mayor

Fiorello La Guardia banned push carts, ostensibly because of safety, since fire engines would not have room to navigate the street in case of a fire. In spite of what I read, Delancy Street and Orchard Street had these push carts in mid-1950's. This was the New York City version of an open-air shopping mall; the closest modern-day equivalent can be seen in Seoul, Singapore or Xian. I hope you are getting a picture of this area of Manhattan in the 1950's.; it was made up of many ethnic populations, for which a church or Synagogue provided a community focal point. The neighborhood was also permeated by symbols of American society such as Vaudeville theatres and movie houses. I don't know how other ethnic groups perceived this neighborhood, but my impression was that we were an island unto ourselves, we were foreigners that didn't mix well with the local Americans or the other immigrants. Perhaps this feeling was self-inflicted since it was up to ourselves to assimilate into the American community. We stuck together with our language and customs which made us feel comfortable, but isolated from the larger community.

I'll conclude this section with a description of 1st Avenue that had food and clothes stores, and restaurants, from First Street up until 14th Street, and this section was a popular shopping destination for the locals. First Avenue is a wide through-street that goes all the way to Harlem, a distance of about 12 miles. Walking north from 7th Street, you'd see some of the stores flow out into the street with their goods on wooden structures that were put up each morning. As an example, I recall an Italian seafood store near 9th street that would display clams, oysters and mussels on top of a bed of ice, on the wooden platform in front of the store window. A customer would walk up and buy a half dozen clams or oysters and eat these raw creatures as he stood in front of the store. I had seen this many times but I could not imagine doing such a thing. Much of the buying of groceries was done on 1st Avenue. Meat was bought at a 'Provisions' Store, with sawdust on the floor and several butchers behind a tall, glass counter that wrapped your purchase in wax-infused paper. You'd see the butcher assemble your order, write the price of each item on a brown paper bag with a black crayon and write the total, without hesitation, right on the bag. Calculator not required. As I think of this now, the sight of a merchant adding and subtracting figures in his head was a daily reminder that arithmetic was important for ordinary life.

Childhood on 7th Street

The Lower East Side, meaning the lower (or southern) east side of Manhattan, i.e. east of Fifth Avenue, and south of 14th Street, bulges out into the East River. Nowadays this area is called the 'East Village,' I presume because it sounds highfalutin, and the lower east side is designated as the area just south of the East Village. The word 'village' was appropriated from the bohemian (Beatnik) community of 'Greenwich Village' which is located west of Fifth Avenue and south of 4th Street. The locals never called our area the East Village, and Greenwich Village was a foreign place to us, although I discovered that I could venture there to smoke without being seen by the Ukrainian adults that may have known me. Greenwich Village is isolated from the Ukrainian community because 6th, 7th, 8th and ninth Streets did not go through to the Village, being separated by factories and warehouses that run along the Bowery. I would venture alone to Washington Square Park, that formed the southern border of 5th Avenue, which contained an amalgam of students from NY University, fashionable New Yorkers and Beatniks, and watch them (the Beatniks), surrounded by a group of tourists and local immigrant kids like me, play bongo drums in whatever spot they found to sit. Often, on the weekend in late afternoon, I would go to the Village Vanguard, a café and well-known beatnik hangout that provided an evening venue for the latest jazz musicians to strut their stuff, for an ice cream sundae. The streets north of 14th were planned in the late 19th century and so were laid out along a Cartesian grid, north-south and east-west. The thoroughfares running north/south are called 'Avenues' and the cross east-west streets are numbered as Streets. The north-south Streets east of 1st Avenue, moving towards the East River are lettered, and Avenue A, the first of the lettered streets, runs from 14th Street to Houston Street (for approximately about a half mile). The other north-south streets were Avenues B, C, and D and each street was a little shorter than the previous one since the 'bulge' in Manhattan turns toward South Ferry. This part of Manhattan came to be called Alphabet City but this was not what we called it during my childhood. The Franklin Delano Roosevelt (FDR) Drive was east of Avenue D and separated East River Park, adjacent to the East River, from the residential areas. Avenue A was and still is a local street, lined with five story tenements and small businesses sporadically located on the first, street-level entrance, except for the two-block distance of Tompkins Square park that runs from 7th to 10th Street. In my day, Avenue A was the transition between the black and Puerto Rican communities and the European immigrants like myself. The north and south boundaries of the lower east side are the Stuyvesant Peter Cooper Village apartments bounded on 14th Street and extending north towards 20th Street, First Avenue and FDR drive, and Houston Street which runs from FDR drive and continues towards the west side to Chinatown. Stuyvesant town was a post-World War II housing project built with private funds in 1946. The buildings are red brick high-rises of about 10 stories with some common grassy areas, and their size distinguished them from the five story tenements where the newly arrived immigrants lived. As immigrants, we thought that Stuyvesant Town was where the 'rich' lived, and locals from the lower (south) streets were not welcome. This area of Manhattan also contains Tompkins Square Park, a grassy area and playground bounded by Avenues A and B, and 7th and 10th Streets, and East River Park that runs between Houston Street and 14th Street, and bounded by FDR Drive and the East River, of about a one block width. Tompkins Square Park was named after Daniel Tompkins, a Governor of New York and United States Vice President who I have read was a corrupt politician, and served as vice president in James Monroe's first term in the 1820s. These two parks were important to the community since this was the only local green space for families to escape their apartments. In my case I played in Tompkins Square Park as a child and, as I grew older, I ventured into and played in East River Park. I'll mention several other things regarding these two parks. Tompkins Square Park was where Dmytro and I played as young boys, since it was close to our apartment and we could get there without supervision. Three quarters of the boundary of the park was enclosed within a 4 to 5-foot high decorative metal fence, with a central grassy area, and in the center, and a ¼ mile circular path for walking or running. The north/western end of the park had a children's playground with a 'monkey gym,' swings, a wading pool, and parallel bars and a high bar, and a paved area used for baseball played with a rubber (Spalding) ball and broomstick handle as the bat. Our brand of baseball was played in the cordoned-off area perpendicular to 10th Street and a steel mesh fence about 20 feet high, intended to prevent a rubber baseball from leaving the park, lined the lower half of the 10th Street boundary. You could play baseball with only three kids: a pitcher, catcher and hitter. There was a public library just opposite this fence, outside of the park, where I discovered The Hardy Boys and Nancy Drew, in my 6th, 7th and 8th grades. I would often visit the library and cart home eight to ten books at a time and finish reading these within the two-week loan period. I also paid many fines in late fees, 5cents per day per book.

The park has gone through many changes in the last sixty years and you may want to read about these in historical accounts. The history that is prominent in my mind includes the period in the 1950's when the park was filled with immigrants, and the period in the 1960's when it degenerated into a place for drugs and homelessness. I have read biographies of Andy Warhol and memoirs by artists such as Bob Dylan and Debbie Harry of Blondie, that had left their own suburban communities, come to live and glamorize our neighborhood, bring with them their freewheeling lifestyles, and drugs. These accounts of this era do not represent me and the Ukrainian community. We considered these 'artists' as intruders who propagated the drug culture and ruined many lives. They could easily have gone back home or to rehab centers, but we didn't have this choice.

The streets east of the park, Avenues C and D, were also not a place where you wanted go in the late 50's and early 60's, especially at night, because the population living there was poorer and the young people more dangerous than other parts of the neighborhood. As I grew older, I, of course, transitioned from the swings and jungle gym areas to that where baseball was played and older kids hung out. This transition included getting street-wise, i.e. learning how to assess your environment, to look for threatening boys on both sides of the street, looking for escape paths and judging dangers. Sometime in the 8th grade and freshman year in high school I ventured over to East River Park, but only during daytime since local gangs of boys would patrol their boundaries to prevent encroachment by outsiders, especially other boys. These avenues ended at FDR Drive which you had to cross via pedestrian bridges that were spaced every four or five blocks. The park subtended the area between FDR drive and the East River and had, among other things, a running track and typical cement benches with wooden seating slats. The benches lined a walkway and faced the river. I once recall going there with my girlfriend, and sitting at one of these benches and carving our names into the bark of a tree. It was safe to bring a girl here during the daytime to avoid embarrassment of being seen by friends, parents or other adults.

I mention one other incident, a fleeting moment of several minutes, that involved East River Park, that has stayed with me all my life. One day, I was passing by the oval running track and saw a young black guy doing sprints and speed drills. He appeared older than me, perhaps in his late teens or early twenties, and I was astonished that this young guy was putting himself through this pain; no one else was there to time or encourage him. He was apparently training and I was amazed and puzzled as to why he was doing this, all alone. The thought crossed my mind that all his effort wouldn't amount to anything since he was a black guy, that there was prejudice against him, and that he had limited possibilities. I couldn't understand where he would use his training. Yet, this didn't seem to matter to him. I have never been able to figure out why this was such a memorable event to me. I imagine that I thought about how he was doing this for himself, for his own reasons, with no need to show off to anyone; perhaps he was being true to himself. I have never forgotten this young man. I hope that he was successful in his life.

I recently read (in 2019) that Mayor de Blasio proposed rebuilding East River Park and removing the greenery to build a berm at the edge of East River as a protection against the damage caused by a hurricane such as occurred with Hurricane Sandy when the neighborhood was flooded. My understanding is that the park would be re-sodded and remain a green area for the locals.

Dmytro and I went to this park even as small children, wheeling a baby carriage with our brothers, John or Nick. I include below a photo of Dmytro and me in East River Park holding John when he was a baby. I like this picture because it shows us showcasing John, and we appear to be having a good time. This picture shows the river on the right and green space on the left, and we are standing in the walkway in between the park and the East River. The two smoke stacks in the background are part of the coal-fired plant of Consolidated Edison and the buildings are the east side structures of Stuyvesant Town.

Figure 25. Dmytro and I with John on the walkway of East River Park. I am holding John who appears to be several months old. The river is to the right in the photo. The smoke stacks are of the Consolidated Edison Company and the buildings are Stuyvesant Village. I presume that my sister Mary took this photo.

Growing up in the Neighborhood

I do not recall when I became aware of my family's dysfunction but it was most likely in the mid-50s when I was about 10years old. Mary, Dmytro and I arrived in the US with our mother and without a father, into an environment where we were locked into a small area of an enormous city of a foreign country. My mother was 28 years old, Babcha was 60 and we children were 9, 5 and 3. We lived in an area of Manhattan where Ukrainians of all strata of society lived; city and country folk that had known each other in Ukraine or Poland, or the DP camps in Germany. I became aware of the differences between myself and other Ukrainians when I played with other kids, for example with the son of Dr. Makarewich, and with George Glut, the son of what I perceived as wealthy Ukrainians, even though I was not at their economic or social level. I was aware of these differences when I went to their homes to play and where I would see couches and living room chairs covered in heavy-duty plastic, and even at an early age could feel their parents and grandparents giving me sideways glances. We didn't have a father in the house, and my mother did not stay home to take care of us children but worked to provide food for the family. We spoke Ukrainian at home, and in the neighborhood, and of course this meant that we thought in Ukrainian. It was many years before I lost the habit of translating English spoken to me into Ukrainian and vice versa.

When we arrived in New York, Mary and I were registered at St. George School while Dmytro remained home with Babcha while my mother worked. At first, the school was around the corner from where we lived, and later we were transferred to a temporary building on ninth Street while a new school was being built to replace the one on 6th and Taras Shevchenko Streets.

We lived on 7th Street near 2nd Avenue for about two years, and after 1955, we moved eight different times because of what I came to perceive as my family's dysfunction. My mother came to have a relationship with Wasyl Bodnar, a DP of similar background to us, and as a result my brothers John and Nick were born in 1954 and 1955. My mother and Wasyl never married and I assume, as a result of their relationship, we moved many times within the enclave of the Ukrainian neighborhood. Besides the apartment on 7th street, the one on 1st Avenue between 10th and 11th Streets and the apartment on 12th Street between Avenues A and B are most prominent to me. I will describe these apartments so you could get a sense of my environment.

I start with the first apartment on 7th Street. The apartment at 59 East 7th Street is particularly vivid in my memory because this was our first 'permanent' apartment where we spent about two years, shortly after arrival at New York. We had moved to another apartment on 5th Street where John was born in 1954 and Nick in 1955, and I was approximately 10 years old. The 7th street apartment was left to my Babcha, but Dmytro and I continued to live there from approximately 1954 to 1957. We children were shuttled back and forth from this apartment to where my mom lived with Wasyl since we looked after our Babcha with her various chronic medical ailments, taking her for periodic visits to Bellevue

Hospital. Bellevue is a public hospital, located on approximately 29th Street between 1st Avenue and the East River, and in the 1950s this is where the poor went for medical treatment. We did not have a phone in the apartment so my Mom and Babcha counted on me, to call the hospital at the local drug store, and make an appointment for her. These visits to Bellevue were usually in the afternoon, during the weekday, so I would be excused from school to travel by bus with Babcha for her appointment. There was usually a long wait in drab, dimly lit waiting rooms, with ceramic tile floors and walls, and metal benches in the hallways. I hated going to Bellevue.

My Babcha was short in height, a little less than 5 feet tall, but a formidable character. She wore a full, waist-high skirt with petticoats that expanded the skirt that extended to the ground. She always wore a kerchief whenever she left the apartment, and she had a full set of upper and lower false teeth. In those days, I assumed that I would also be toothless when I got to be 55 or 60 years old. One sign of Babcha's status to me was her purchase of black, leather, knee-high boots which she had made by a cobbler in our neighborhood, shortly after we arrived in Manhattan. These boots were a status symbol that indicated a prosperous farmer and she was very proud of having them made. Babcha was our caregiver since my mom worked. She is the one I remember best from these early years in Manhattan. She told us children Fairy Tales, such as Ivasic Telesic (Johnny Telesik) with the lesson being to not go too far from your home, warned us about wolves that were major predators in the 'old country,' and nursed me when I was sick by giving me a shot of brandy mixed in warm milk.

My mother was a little over 5 feet tall, strong-willed and stubborn. The clash of their personalities was inevitable and she and Babcha appeared to my child's eye to have a contentious yet cooperative relationship. My mother listened reluctantly to Babcha but she, my mother, was the breadwinner in the family and so commanded a certain level of respect. My mother also dressed in a blouse and full-length skirt, and wore a kerchief when she went out of doors. I assume that it was the birth of John and Nick that prompted her to move out of the 7th Street apartment, and there must have been some agreement between them that left Dmytro and I to continue living with Babcha.

This apartment on 7th street was at the center of the Ukrainian section and a typical tenement residence as shown in the figure I've included. This building did not have the 'modern conveniences' of central heat or indoor toilet facilities. The steps inside the building were wooden, creaky and bowed, and lit by a light bulb at around the midpoint of the stairwell. Each floor hallway contained two toilets, each enclosed in its own small closet. One toilet was shared by the front two and one by the back two apartments. The hallway was also poorly lit by a single light bulb that seemed to be constantly burned out. The toilet, contained a commode with a water tank situated high up on the wall, and the commode was flushed by pulling a wire chain. You can imagine that going inside this room was a scary proposition especially for young kids who always imagined a bogy man sitting in there as you opened the door.

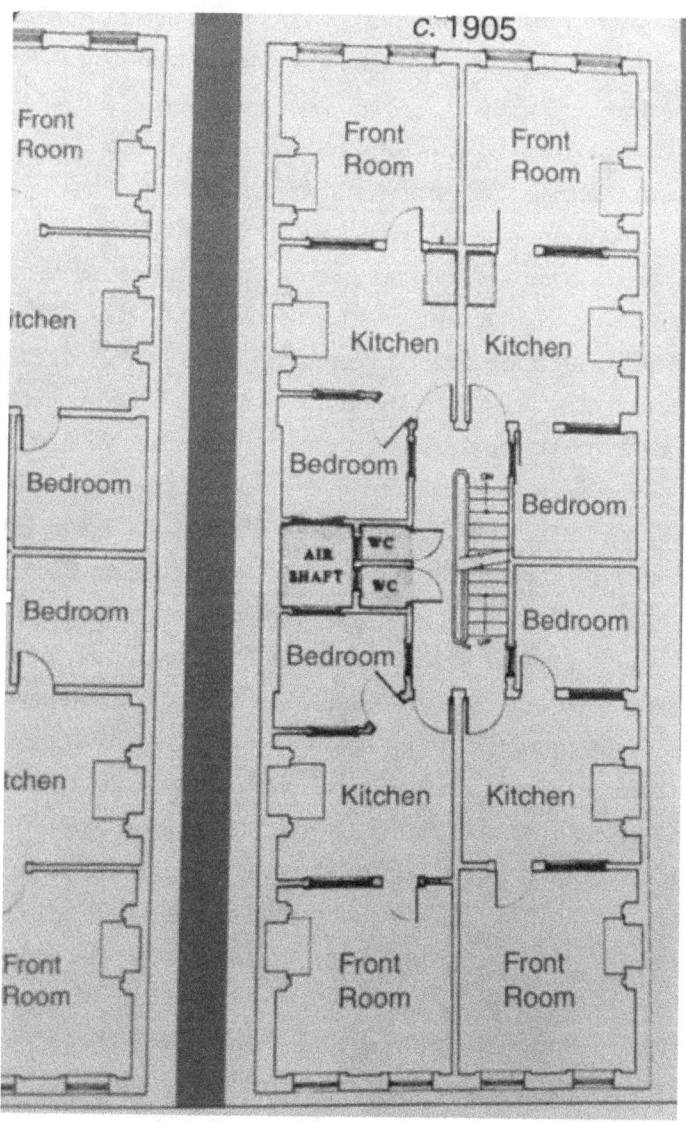

Figure 26. Schematic diagram of a typical floor of apartments, obtained from the book: 97 Orchard Street, New York, that I have referenced at the end of these memoirs. The layout is exactly the same as I remember of the apartment on 59 East 7th Street. This figure shows four apartments and we occupied the apartment at the bottom right.

You entered into the kitchen, with a small bedroom to the left as you entered the apartment. The 'front room' also served as sleeping quarters, with the view from the windows of the back yard. Note the two 'wc's" which stand for water closets and the airshaft located in the hallway between the apartments.

Our apartment was at the back of the building, on the 3rd floor, facing the back yard. You enter into the linoleum-covered kitchen with a bath tub to the right of the door. The tub was covered with an enamel-coated steel metal plate with folded-over edges, and a (Franklin) potbellied stove stood opposite the tub. In the winter, the apartment was kept warm by stoking the stove with coal until the outside of the 'pot' was red hot, before going to bed. The fire burnt down until morning when coal was again thrown into the fire. The top of the metal plate on the bathtub usually covered the top of the tub and was used for food preparation. It was our kitchen island. The potbellied stove was the only source of heat and in the winter, telephone books (the 4-inch thick type), yellow pages (the old-fashioned equivalent of the internet) listing businesses, and newspapers were used as starter material, the wood obtained from wooden crates that were found in the street, and coal which was bought from trucks or horse drawn wagons. I would sometimes be asked by mom or Babcha to get the wood which I found on my wanderings through the streets. This was not difficult since as I've already said many of the streets around Delancy and Orchard Streets had businesses that operated during the daytime and their refuse was empty wood crates, which initially contained produce or fruit, strewn about. There was a small bedroom to the left as you entered and a living room/bedroom on the right of the kitchen facing the back yard. There was a table in front of the potbellied stove and a gas stove to the right of it. I don't remember the location of the kitchen sink but this was where the dishes and sometimes clothes were washed in a tub washer. Outside the living room windows, facing north, was a fire-escape. The sash of the living room window had a pulley attached to it and a rope strung to another pulley attached to a utility pole located at the boundary of our back yard, about 50 feet away, with that of the opposing building. This rope spanned the back yard of our building. The wet laundry was hung with wooden clothes pins on the line and moved along by way of the two pulleys. This was our laundry line and Saturday was laundry time. Across the yard was another back yard with its accompanying tenement, and our two tenements faced each other across these two yards. If you've ever seen Alfred Hitchcock's movie Rear Window you'd recognize the back yard in that movie as similar to what I am describing. You can also get a good sense of the environment from the 1940's comedic movies showing the Bowery Boys. You could see into the apartment opposite your own, and I played Peeping Tom, going so far as to get a telescope, when I reached the age of puberty, so that I could catch a glimpse of a woman that lived across the way who cleaned her apartment in her underwear. The back yards were usually filled with clothes lines and, on any given day you'd see many of the tenant's laundry visible for inspection. I recall sleeping in the living room which also functioned as a bedroom, in a bed that was covered by a feather comforter and a blue-enamel clad metal chamber pot, with cover, about 12 inches in diameter, under the headboard of the bed and, I did sometimes, in the middle of the night, use the chamber pot. This room contained one traditional bed with a huge feather comforter, another vestige of the life my Babcha brought over from her village, and a convertible trundle bed that functioned as a couch in the daytime. The trundle bed converted to a two-mattress sleeping area. Bath time was on the weekend with the metal top of the tub lifted and latched to the wall.

The apartment had an 'icebox,' the inside kept cool by a block of ice purchased from a vendor who drove a horse drawn wagon on the street once or twice a week. This is another of those instances where you'd think we were living in the 19th or early part of the 20th century instead of the middle of the 20th century. When you needed ice, you hailed an ice wagon and the driver delivered the ice by grabbing it with large pincers, placing it on his shoulder and walking up the stairs to your apartment. Of course, it was the children's job to empty a catch tray of the melt, and this was always a bit of contention as to whose turn it was to do this. I recall a cost of 50 cents for a block of ice (18x12x12 inches) and I recently had a discussion with Jack Albright (age 89 in 2019) about this and he told me that he and his father delivered ice in the 1930's in California to military barracks via truck and they charged 25 cents for a 20-lb. block. This was my environment and I'm sure that the people living in the brownstone homes, just several blocks away, had much better accommodations and had little idea of how we lived.

In my home in the early 50s, breakfast consisted of bread and butter and eggs, although dry grain cereal such as Cheerios found its way into my diet after a time. Oftentimes in preparation for school, if time was short, I would be given an egg or two to drink before going out the door. Sometimes dinner was a simple affair with some chicken soup and I recall a number of times eating a plate of bread soaked in warm milk. On Sundays or holidays, I recall Babcha or Mom making boiled chicken which they bought freshly killed at a market on First Avenue. They plucked the feathers and burned off the stubs on the gas stove, the smell of which is still etched into my brain. On special occasions, we ate borsch (a beet soup), pirohy (potatoes and cheese dumplings boiled in water) and holubchi (cabbage stuffed with rice, pork and tomatoes and cooked for hours in an oven). Kowbasy was a ready-to-eat meat sausage which was sometimes available, and we sometimes had fried beef. I was not fond of either the chicken soup or the well-done fried beef. After a time, Babcha also allowed us children to purchase sweets at the local grocer located several doors down the street, on her account. These included fruit pies, what they call fried pie here in the south, Little Debbies, Yoo Hoo and other such packaged dessert. The proprietor of the store knew us kids and we'd go in, pick an item from the counter, show it to him, and run back out. He kept track of these purchases and my Babcha or mom would pay for these items when the next payday came along. In those days, there was a deposit charged on bottles of soft drinks, two cents for each bottle, and oftentimes I would go on a hunt to find theses glass bottles and use the change buy more drinks. Another store that I frequented sold comic books, new ones for 10 cents, with the possibility to trade it in for a used one for 2 cents. I liked the Superman comics and especially the science articles, about the solar system, galaxies, and comets, that were interspersed between the stories of superman. It is hard for me to imagine that a store owner could have made a living selling comic books.

We did not have a television set in these early years and I recall trying to get myself invited to an apartment in my building so that I could watch cowboy movies, Gene Autry, Hopalong Cassidy or the Lone Ranger. When we finally did acquire a TV set, My Babcha loved to watch 'professional wrestling' and she would curse like a longshoreman whenever her favorite wrestler was losing his match. We bought a TV set in the late 1950s and it was my job to keep it running by checking the vacuum tubes. I learned early on how to remove the back panel of the set and pull out the tubes, take these to the local drug store that had a 'tube checker' and buy a new tube. It seemed that our TV had very low reliability, and you could never be sure which tube was the one that prevented the set from working, so naturally you took all the tubes out for checking. You can't appreciate how frustrating this was, especially since the set was breaking down very often. You need to appreciate the strides made in the reliability of electronics over the decades.

I prepared for school by dressing in dark pants, a white shirt and navy blue tie and then walking to church for Mass. After Mass, I'd walk to the school building around the corner. My clothing was a uniform of sorts, so from very early age I was wearing a coat and necktie to school. Basilian Nuns taught us penmanship, English, arithmetic, geography and history, and, we had religious instruction by a priest. The nuns spoke to us in English. We were also taught to save our nickels and dimes in paper coin-folds that had an inset big enough for the coin, which we then submitted, in class, to a person representing a Credit Union. As a characteristic of the time, we had been issued dog tags to wear around our necks and practiced hiding under our desks during weekly drills, in case the Soviet Union dropped an atomic bomb on New York.

The church in my child's view was a majestic structure which you entered by ascending about twenty steps, the inside of the building being a two-story structure with a balcony on three sides. The altar area was partially screened by several partitions that had icons of the saints similar to what you might see in a Greek Orthodox church, except that the partition did not totally block the altar from the congregation. On Sunday mornings, High Mass was celebrated at 10am and the responses sung by the congregants and a choir situated at the rear balcony. These choir and congregant responses were in Church Slavonic, an ancient form of Ukrainian which is still used in Ruthenian churches. I did not like going to High Mass since I thought it was very long, with the choir stretching out every 'Kyrie' into a several minute refrain. If you've ever listened to Mozart's Requiem you'll understand what I mean. The basement of the church was used for overflow crowds during special holidays, social events of societies like the Society of the Blessed Virgin Mary, etc., and supplemental religious instruction for the boys and girls preparing for Holy Communion. While I was in first and second grade, my time consisted of going to Mass every day before school, and preparing to receive Holy Communion.

The sacrament of confession and reception of First Holy Communion was a right-of-passage of every child at around 7 years old and it involved getting instruction in the sacraments, with confession heard by a priest. My only recollection of one of these lectures, in preparation for confession, and his talk, giving an example of a sin. The priest said that writing with a (lead) wooden pencil and then touching the point of the pencil to your tongue was a sin. I sat there wondering why this was a sin and several of us children discussed this 'sin' after his talk. None of us could figure out what this meant.

The First Communion pageantry was something very special. It was especially so since in the Ukrainian Church of the Byzantine Slovanic Rite, Confirmation is done during Baptism, so the receipt of Holy Communion was the next big right-of-passage at this crucial stage of a child's life. Families were excited to have their children reach this particular milestone and generally the family hosted a meal or had a family gathering with friends at home after the ceremony. The First Communion Reception was at a special Mass where the boys were dressed in dark suits with a white shirt and navy pants, and the girls in white dresses and white stockings and shoes. The boy's shirt had a stiff, detachable collar, with broadly rounded corners, and a huge white-ribbon tie finished off the look. Each child was given a candle for a procession, boy and girl combinations, walking down the main aisle of the church, and, after Mass, I recall getting a medallion and a remembrance card of my First Holy Communion in 1953. These items, collar, tie, candle and medallion, were placed in a box (a cigar box or something like it) and stored on top of a clothes bureau in our apartment. I lost track of these items after Dorothea and I were married, except for the remembrance card. The church was the center of life in our community; everything revolved around holidays and ceremonies at the church, and as I grew older I became an altar boy.

I will mention one other memory of church which stands out to me and which will seem unusual to you, and that is one of the religious ceremonies during lent. Easter is the most solemn holiday in the church calendar and Lent was known as a time for fasting, especially the week before Easter. For example, meat was not eaten all week, and Monday, Wednesday and Friday dairy was not allowed in addition to no meat. During Holy Week, the church was decorated with a make-shift sarcophagus, the bottom of which is placed at a 12-inches height off the floor, and topped with a pergola covered with cloth. The sarcophagus was at the front of the church, near the alter, and during the week, the congregants would enter the church by kneeling just inside the church doors and crawling on hands and knees up to the image of a shroud of the dead Jesus laying inside the 'burial tomb.' The kneeling congregant would kiss the shroud, then skooch sideways to make room for the next worshiper. This went on all week until Saturday when the sarcophagus was taken down in preparation for the Resurrection Service on Easter Sunday. While fasting was going on, a sumptuous meal was prepared on Friday, then taken to church on Saturday, in a wicker basket, to be blessed, for consumption after Mass. This meal consisted of a bread/cake called paska, boiled eggs, ham, and a beets and horseradish condiment. Dorothea has continued to make this meal, for my sake, and our family has eaten this Easter Sunday meal since our marriage. I mention these religious rights and feasts to give you some indication of how the Church was central to my life at this time.

St. George School

I was registered into 1st grade, at five years old, in the fall just after we arrived in the US. My recollection of those early years is of practicing cursive writing, learning English, and being taught the multiplication tables. Besides English we also learned how to read and write in Ukrainian. I still remember while in second or third grade, I was excited to figure out that multiplication is based on addition and I didn't need to memorize the tables. School also meant that we learned lessons in class, then we had homework, which I did as soon as possible when I got home. We also sang in class, by standing as a group next to our seats, songs such as the Star-Spangled Banner and America the Beautiful. I liked hands-on projects, such as, for example, the creation of posters that needed meticulously measured and spaced letters and the making of clay models of 16th century native American (the Iroquois nation) life in villages, of a scale to fit inside a cigar box. These were projects started in class and it was expected that we would finish these at home. Children in those days were also taught Civics, which included information on the industry and the geography of New York State. For example, I still remember learning that in the 17th and 18th century, New York had a large dairy and leather industry, and local companies manufactured shoes, coats and hats for local consumption as well as export. Besides classroom learning, the nuns took us on occasional outings to Central Park to visit the zoo, and, the Museum of Natural History, and the Planetarium. It was amazing to see huge skeletons of whales magically suspended in the air, and to walk past Mastodons in the Central Hall. What a space, it was mesmerizing. The museum had stuffed giraffes, Ibex, deer, lions and tigers, and wax figures of cave men and women dressed in animal skins pretending to kill animals. This scene of ancient humans dressed in animal skins in a museum is shown tongue-in-cheek in the movie, "*Planet of the Apes*", where in this case, real humans are 'stuffed' and on view to the apes. I assume this scene was written into the script of the movie by Rod Serling, a New Yorker and screen writer of the *Twilight Zone* and of *The Planet of the Apes*, who must have remembered going to this museum. The mineral collection was mind blowing.

My memory of the early grade-school years is that I was disruptive in class and told to kneel in the corner of the classroom as punishment for some infraction or other, as opposed to being sent to the Principals office for detention as is done these days. I got into fights with other boys and I was the dominant boy in the first, second and third grades. My bullying ended after the fourth grade when the other boys began to outgrow me in height and weight. During these years, I had my nose broken three times.

I will mention three other memories that stand out in the temporary school on 9th Street. Grade school was strict and punishment included getting slapped on the hands with a rubber strap. I recall one time of being called to the Principles office for some offense of which I was not guilty and being told to hold out my hand to receive my punishment. If you withdrew your hand then you got a double whack. My other memory is of the recesses which were during lunchtime in a yard outside the building. The boys played punch ball most days, but sometimes we ended up listening to one of our classmates, Leo Chalupa, tell stories of Cowboys and Indians. He was a wonderful spinner of tales, describing the scenery and characters with such vividness that the images of these characters in your minds' eye was as real as could be, and all the boys crowded around him trying to catch every word. We didn't want to go back inside the building.

My description above sounds like that of a typical kid except that I realized that my family was different from other families because I didn't have a father. I recognize now that I must have been depressed about the loss of my father but I did not show it outwardly except by my belligerent behavior toward other boys. I don't ever recall talking about the death of my father with my Mom or Mary or Dmytro and I wish we all would have been encouraged to do this. It seemed to me that everyone came from nice, perfect families with a mother, father and children except in our family, there was my mother and Babcha, and us children. What further distressed me were arguments between my mother and Babcha and the eventual association of my mother with Wasyl Bodnar. I will not describe his background except to say that he was also a Ukrainian immigrant and must have been as traumatized as the other immigrants by going through the war. This association of my mother with Wasyl Bodnar in the period of 1950-1955 was what caused our family to move our residence, even to Philadelphia, and then move within the neighborhood several more times. There was silence as to the death of my father and this silence led to feelings of abandonment, and shame that we were different. Even though I'm sure we all felt this shame, we never discussed it. This awkward feeling of shame and difference carried over into my relationship with my siblings, friends and their parents. It felt to me that everyone knew that we were fatherless and that everyone felt sorry for us. I had the feeling that some people looked on us as orphans.

I also felt that my mother's relationship with Wasyl Bodnar was known to the Ukrainian community and that this relationship caused my mother to be ostracized and criticized by them. I believe that it was this ostracism of my mother that led to the move to Philadelphia. As I've gotten older I've come to appreciate the value of discussing difficult events in ones' life in spite of the pain.

Many years later, my mother reconciled with the Ukrainian community. She joined church organizations, made many friends and even used her cross-stitching talents to embroider an alter cloth and priest vestments for the parish. These items are currently displayed at the Ukrainian Museum on 6th Street, around the corner from the church.

Sometime during the 1950's, prior to and after we stayed in Philadelphia, my mom and we children moved in with Wasyl Bodnar and I was very confused as to who he was in relation to me. I say we moved in with Wasyl Bodnar but I don't have any memory of actually moving and leaving my Babcha at the apartment on 7th Street. As I've stated above, there must have been an agreement between my mom and Babcha to let us children continue to live on 7th street until 1957. Besides the silence about the death of my father, there was silence about my mother's relationship with Wasyl Bodnar. At one point I was asked by my mom to call him 'Dad,' and when I objected, I was told to call him 'uncle.' This period in my life was filled with confusion since Dmytro and I were disciplined by Wasyl and we resented it. I could not understand my mothers' decision to move all of us and to become separated from Babcha. I later came to understand and appreciate how my Mom would need to have a partner to provide resources to a household and education for her kids with the hope of escaping the neighborhood, but, even as I got older with a family of my own, I never discussed with her the idea of having two more children. My mom must have loved Wasyl and she no doubt needed love as a young woman, she was about 30 years old at this time.

It was during this period that I came to be angry with my mom and came to resent her decision of moving herself and us children in with Wasyl. Of course, I loved my mom but this anger was there and it wasn't until I was in my 20s, married and with Christine that I came to grips with it. My Babcha also had a lot to say about this association of my Mom and Wasyl. I recall many fights between my mom and Babcha but I can't remember what these fights were about. My Babcha was the mother-in-law, and this must have exacerbated the strain in their relationship. The apartment was always in a state of tension with Babcha yelling and berating our Mom. So, besides my Babcha, we kids resented Wasyl and, in retrospect, I cannot imagine what he could have done or what my mother might have said to make us accept him into our lives. This relationship was a dead end for all concerned.

Figure 27. Photo of our 'family': my mom, Mary, me and Dmytro, including Wasyl Bodnar. I remember those winter jackets and the fact that Dmytro and I dressed as twins. This photo must have been taken before the birth of John in 1954.

We made every effort to appear normal to the outside world, going through daily life, and hiding our true feelings. During these early years, my mom tried to make ends meet by working at several jobs; for example, at a Rope Factory in Brooklyn just where the Williamsburg Bridge crosses the East River, then at the Harts

Mountain Bird Seed factory on 4th Avenue and 6th Street. I am not aware what she actually did at these factories but I assume hers were menial jobs since she could not read or write in English.

Figure 28. Photo of Mary, me and Dmytro in the early 1950s. I am to Mary's right. I believe this was in Tompkins Square Park.

Some more details of St. George School

Grade school generally takes over the lives of young children, and this is what I felt about St. George School in the early 50s. It seems like the entire day is taken up with school and the balance of the day is used to recuperate from the day. St. George School was initially located at the corner of East 6th and Taras Shevchenko Streets and in 1953 the parish decided to build a new school in its place. The school was moved into a temporary building on 9th Street and Avenue C at about the time of the World Series in 1955, when the Yankees played the victorious Brooklyn Dodgers. The radio-announced final game was piped into the classrooms via the public-address system, and this was the first time that I became aware of baseball. Years later Dmytro and I would sneak into Yankee stadium to watch Yogi Berra, Whitey Ford, Mickey Mantle and Roger Maris play ball. Mary, Dmytro and I walked from our Babcha's apartment to this building while the new school was being built. Our teachers were nuns, with a few lay teachers and occasionally a parish priest filling in some of the classes. For most of my grade-school years, the classes were segregated by sex, i.e. separate boy's and girl's classes until 1956 after which the classes became co-educational. The classes were taught in English, however, there was one hour spent on Ukrainian lessons (I include here a photo of one Ukrainian class, with Dmytro and me sitting in the front row in our plaid shirts). The switching back and forth from Ukrainian to English and visa-versa is the usual case with multilingual families. However, the unwritten contract between the immigrants and their adopted country is that the immigrant is expected to learn the language, accept the cultural norms, and assimilate into society. If you live in a ghetto where your native language and customs are all you know, you'll be isolated from the larger community and in danger of not advancing economically or participating in society. If you purposely stay isolated, then you are not living up to your part of this bargain. It is usually much harder for the older generation to assimilate because their learning skills are slower, and so my mother and Babcha depended on us children to assimilate for them. They placed their hopes for becoming American on us children.

Figure 29. Photo of my mom, John, Mary and Dmytro in East River Park which I took with my Kodak Brownie camera, circa 1956 or 1957.

My Brother Dmytro

In the period of 1950 to 1955 Dmytro and I were inseparable and I took it on myself to protect him and show him the ropes. In those days he was called Jimmy, a name suggested by Nick Kunitsky who thought an American sounding name would be easier on him in America. Dmytro and I were very similar in stature and many times were taken for twins. In the summer, we played together and had great fun roaming the neighborhood. 'Go out and play, and be sure to come back before dinner' was the typical instruction that moms gave kids in those days. When not in school, we generally spent all day playing in the neighborhood, and when we got home, we were told to wash our hands, face and necks. Why neck I could never figure out. We played in the streets around the tenements, sometimes in the separation space between buildings, and in the back yards, by ourselves or with other boys. You have to be creative when you don't have money to buy toys. One particular memory of our creativity is discovering the Wanamaker store near our residence, between 9th and 10th Streets, and Broadway and Fourth Avenue.

Figure 30. 1950's photo of the John Wanamaker store on 9th Street and 4th Avenue.

Wanamaker's is the name of a wealthy business family from Philadelphia that built high-end stores in the northeast of the US and they had several stores in NYC. The one near our apartment, was situated in two multi-story buildings connected via a bridge across 9th Street, somewhat like the Marshall Fields' store in Chicago was a few years ago. I include a photo of the building above. We would walk to the store and play in the aisles of the toy section on the 3rd floor, riding the tricycles and bicycles, and miniature electric cars up and down the aisles, and generally make pests of ourselves. The store clerks would eventually chase us out when they realized that we were unaccompanied by adults. Wanamaker's also had special events in the toy department, one of which I recall had a 'live' baby elephant cordoned off in a section with hay strewn about. This was definitely for the hoi paloi and this is how we amused ourselves whenever we got the chance.

Figure 31. Photo of a grade school class in which Ukrainian was taught. The ages of the children were mixed and you'll notice Dmytro and me in the front row table wearing our plaid shirts.

John and Nick

John and Nick came into our lives in 1954 and 1955, when I was 10 years old. As I've already mentioned, Mary, Dmytro and I played with them and provided some level of care but as usual with a child that is 10 years younger than you, you don't interact with them until both they and you are more fully grown. In this case, this didn't occur until they were enrolled in St. George school at about 5 years old, and I was further removed from interacting with them. I started high school in 1959, so as a teenager, I didn't want the responsibility of their care. Besides I was into my own life at this time. I chalk this up to my remembering little of their upbringing. We knew that John was very smart in grade school, and the Nick was very good with technical things; I don't remember interacting with them until Dorothea and I were married, and we had Christine.

Mary

Mary is my older sister so by definition we fought when we were younger. My first memory of her was at the apartment on Avenue A, where we stayed when we first arrived in the US, when I was 5 years old. My one recollection of her was her cleaning of this apartment, and forbidding Dmytro and I to walk into the living room and sit on the couch, just after she cleaned it. Of course, this got me mad and I complained to mom and snuck into the living room just to make her angry. Of course, Mary lived with us on 7th Street but I don't remember her from this period. My next memory of Mary was her going to Julia Richmond High School for her freshman year, 1956-1957, and in the sophomore year moving to a boarding school, staffed by Ukrainian Basilian nuns in Fox Chase, just north of Philadelphia. Mary became a 'Juniorate' in preparation to becoming a 'novitiate' after which she entered the convent in 1960. I also recall discussion of her going to the convent and arguments between Babcha and Mom of trying to talk her out of this decision. Mary is stubborn and so she went. During the three years of 1958-1960, she returned home during holidays, while I attended the sixth, seventh and eighth grade.

We all missed Mary, and I remember Dmytro and I competing for her attention when she came home for these visits, sometimes with her novitiate girlfriends. The family made many visits to Fox Chase and there were several times when as a twelve-year old my mother asked me to visit Mary with several 'shopping' bags of food, clothes and other items. I went by way of a subway to the Port Authority, travelling to New Jersey and catching the Pennsylvania Rail Road at Union Station in Newark, to North Philadelphia. I caught the North Philadelphia bus to Fox Chase, the location of the high school, and walked the final leg of this trip. Today, it seems inconceivable that a parent would send a 12-year old boy from NYC to Philadelphia assuming that I would have the wherewithal to find my way there and return. My mother had great confidence in me, and I had confidence that I could do this.

It was also in this time period that I became fascinated with electric motors and I built several using diagrams I had seen in books. An electric motor contains a commutator, stator and rotor, each wound with insulated wire and plugged into a power outlet to create electromagnets of the windings. I'll leave it to you to investigate how this is done. At the time of this experiment, I did not know that many miles of *thin* gauge, insulated wire are needed to create the strength in the electromagnet to turn the windings. I built my first electric motor with thick gauge wire several feet long, too thick for the size and scale of this experiment, mounted the electromagnets on a wooden board, and attached the 120-volt plug to the ends of the wires of the stator and inserted this plug into the wall. Of course, this experiment ended in disaster since I short-circuited the entire building and burned out the compressor of our refrigerator. Although I believe my mother knew that I had caused this chaos in the building, she never brought it up. The building was out of power for the day and we needed to get a new refrigerator. This was the end of my experiments in building electric motors.

As I grew older living at the 1st Avenue apartment, I somehow lost contact with my Babcha; I visited her less and less and did not stay with her at the 7th Street address. Her health deteriorated and after a stay in a hospital, she was transferred to a nursing home where she died in 1966. My sad memory of the funeral Mass is of Pan Kunitsky coming up to me with a somber, sad face, with hat in hand, and extending his hand to me to offer his condolences. It's hard to describe this emotional encounter with him, however, I'll always remember that he approached me as the oldest male in our family to offer condolences. This was also the last time that I saw Pan Kunitsky. He died in 1968.

Pre-teens on 1st Avenue

In the time period of 1955 to 1960, after my mom gave birth to John and Nick, she quit her factory job and took a job as a 'super' i.e. superintendent of a tenement, taking care of keeping the building clean and functioning. We moved into an apartment on 1st Avenue, between 10th and 11th Streets, on the east side of the street. John and Nick's father worked as an elevator operator in a high-rise office building in midtown Manhattan so the arrangement was that my mom would take care of the building, such as sweeping and washing the floors and keeping the boiler stoked, then she would go to her evening job when their father came home from his job. This arrangement helped with the finances of our family.

The responsibilities of the 'super' included the feeding and stoking of the boiler for hot water and steam heat, reporting serious issues to the building owner, and sweeping and mopping the floors for free rent. My mom and Wasyl took on this responsibility, but it fell to my mother to carry out the duties of the 'super' during the daytime while Wasyl worked. My mom's evening job was that of a 'cleaning lady' in downtown Manhattan, on second shift, starting at 4pm. Mom left for her evening job at about 3:15 and Wasyl got home at about 5:30, so it was up to Mary, Dmytro and I to fill in this time of care for John and Nick. My mom's job was to clean six or seven floors, on Broad Street in the Wall Street area of Manhattan, and a number of times I went with her. I helped clean the toilets and sinks, and empty out the wastebaskets.

The 1st Avenue apartment was a typical four room flat, on the first floor at street level, and located towards the back of the building. We were the only ones at ground level and the apartment had a bedroom to the right as you entered into the kitchen. As usual, the floors were linoleum but this apartment had an inside toilet, a luxury compared to what I was used to. This tenement did not have a stoop and upon entering the building you walked past a stairway toward the back of the building where you found our door. I mention this detail because the building front door was not locked, and there were instances when opening the door of our apartment, in the morning, we'd sometimes find a homeless or drunken man sleeping in front of our door. We would wake this man and try to get him to leave. The side of the stairway had a door that led to the basement where the boiler was located, and the basement was partitioned into smaller bins used for coal storage. Coal was delivered to the building by trucks that dumped the coal into the manhole in the sidewalk in the front of the building. This access to the tenement basement is still there today, and I sometimes wonder if people walking past buildings realize the reason these manhole covers are there. This huge pile of coal needed to be moved to a bin closer to the boiler, so that shoveling it into the boiler was easier, and at times I moved the coal by shoveling it into a wheelbarrow and moving the coal. You can imagine that it was particularly important to never let the fire die down since if this happened, it was time-consuming to get the fire started, and the building would have no heat or hot water for a period of time. This was a years' long job since hot water is needed throughout the year. Throwing shovelfuls of coal into that boiler was a job I had during the evenings when my mom was at work. My mom would sometimes hire a derelict to move this coal and she learned early on to never pay them until they had finished the job because there were a number of times when they skipped out if they had been paid beforehand. It was then up to us, and me personally, to move the coal.

Figure 32. Photo of a celebration dinner for Mary, when she finished being a 'postulant' and received her 'habit,' and the start of her two-year period as a 'novitiate.' The picture shows my mom with Nick sitting on her knee, Babcha with the kerchief, and Pani Kunitsky among the women and girls. The lone man in the background is Mykola Mykolyn, a close personal friend from as far back as the DP camps. I don't know the names of the others.

Stress on First Avenue

My memory of this apartment is of mom and Wasyl arguing, especially when he came home drunk, but I never understood why they fought or what the fights were about. Sometimes the neighbors called the police, but I recall many times when mom became hysterical and in the mayhem, yelled to me to call the police. Since we didn't have a phone in the apartment, I would run to the corner phone booth, call and wait until the police arrived. The police then escorted him out of the apartment. It was during these years that my mom depended on me for support and I tried to do the best I could. In some way, I was her ticket out of her situation.

You can imagine that my adolescence on 1st Avenue was very stressful because of the fighting between my mom and Wasyl, and the commotion this caused in the household. Even as a young boy, I asked my mom many times to separate from Wasyl but she couldn't or wouldn't do this. As to the fights, there was nothing I could do.

Figure 33. My high school graduation picture in 1959.

Realities of Living in an Apartment

One of the realities of living in an apartment building, in a large city, is dealing with the problem of roaches and rodents. Roaches were everywhere, concentrated in the kitchen, and you needed to be careful where you stepped at night when the lights were out. These pests were searching for food in the sink or dish cabinets and you quickly learned to check a cup or glass before filling with water or milk. I am still in the habit of doing this. I had learned to sweep the floor at night before going to bed because of the possibility of stepping on a roach in the middle of the night in case I needed to go to the bathroom. There is nothing to be done with roaches, they were everywhere, and you needed to get used to them. Rodents were also a big problem, and I have had a number of experiences with rats at the 1st Avenue apartment. One particularly amusing and victorious incident, at least amusing from this distance of time, is my battling a rat that got into the kitchen from underneath the sink. This particular incident was sometime before midnight, before my mother came home from her second shift job. The rat bore its way into the kitchen by chewing a hole in the wall beneath the sink, and pulling the garbage bag near to the hole so that it could easily get at the garbage. All his rustling woke me and I realized that I would need to plug his hole or this would go on all night. I spent several hours plugging the hole with Plaster of Paris that I learned to mix. You need to imagine me stirring the plaster in a bucket, filling the hole as fast as I could with the nose of the rat visible to me. I eventually succeeded by using every last bit of a five-pound bag stuffed into the hole. Although the rat continued eating and gnawing through the wet plaster, it finally hardened faster than he could digest it and he gave up. This was one small victory that I have never forgotten. I have recently read that NYC is currently having (in 2019) an infestation of rats, so this problem has not gone away

Cultural Changes in the 50's and early 60's

There were enormous cultural changes occurring in the US in the 1950s and 1960s. I will mention those events that I especially remember or that had particular meaning to me. The cold war was constantly in the news, with Germans in Berlin escaping into West Germany and being killed in the process. At the same time, imagine what the war in Korea and the development of atomic weapons by the Soviets caused in our community. As I've already mentioned, I recall the historic announcement on the front pages of the New York Daily News of Stalin's death in 1953, and the joy in our community at his death. This talk of communism caused a persistent anxiety in me even though I was just 8 years old. Other developments at this time include the Soviet launch of sputnik in 1957 and the uproar that the US was falling behind in the arms race. My neighborhood was also very concerned about the ultimatum issued by President Kennedy during the Cuban Crisis, in 1961, and I recall that evening when the entire world was waiting on news of the location of the Soviet ships headed to Cuba. Would the Soviet ships, with missiles on board, turn back? Even though I was a young teenager at this time, my friends and I talked about the possibility of war, and anxiously waited for this event to play out. So, even though I was in my early teens, my life in the neighborhood was surrounded by fear of these wide-ranging national and geopolitical issues. On a more personal level, the 1950's saw periodic episodes of infectious diseases such as measles, rubella, and polio. Our generation lived through these infectious diseases and we waited for the development of anti-viral drugs and vaccines, much like we are doing now with the coronavirus pandemic. The medical community knew that another episode of polio was going to occur in 1953, but there was nothing to be done about it. Everyone was frightened, children did not go out to play. Polio struck several children in our school; one of my classmates was paralyzed in his legs and he was a daily reminder of polio in our midst. I recall TV news showing children in heart-lung machines and of finally seeing pictures of President Eisenhower presenting the Congressional Gold Metal to Dr. Salk in 1955 for the discovery of the polio vaccine. In this same time period, other anti-viral drugs for measles, and rubella were discovered. It is beyond the scope of my memoirs to say any more beyond just mentioning these select items but I hope you get the sense of how children were impacted by this news.

I have already mentioned the changes that took place in the 1960s but I was reminded of the law and order, race relations, drugs and protests in New York and especially our neighborhood during this era from the book, *Hardhat Riot, Nixon, New York City and the Dawn of the White Working Class Revolution* by David Paul Huhn. Kuhn reports on the year 1968 and 1969, at the height of the Vietnam war protests but I recall the years leading up to this time. He quotes Edmund White, a Village Voice reporter, "Uncollected garbage piled up along the curb. The sidewalks were cracked and tilted by tree roots. Streetlights were burned out and weren't replaced. The crime rate was high. Burglaries were so common that no one paid much attention to them except the victims...When I moved to Rome in 1970, I suggested to an Italian friend that we switch sides of the street to avoid confronting three teenagers coming toward us. We were always aware of everyone in our immediate vicinity...We made sure we had at least twenty dollars with us every time we left home so that a robber wouldn't shoot us in frustration, but were also careful not to carry more-nor to be too well dressed". My mom followed these rules, hiding a twenty dollar bill in her bra and this came in handy the several times she was mugged in the hallway at the entrance to her building. This was our existence and we prided ourselves in knowing the rules to stay alive. This chaos in 1968 was building at the start of the 60s.

Teenage Friends

Bear, Johnny Uke, Red, Fatty, Rusty, Torchy, Fatso, Big Stevie, Fats, Al Murgo, and Richy D'Amico. These are the names of the group of boys I hung around with, and was influenced by. My nickname was either 'little Stevie' or 'Danny,' because Big Steve was Steve Atamanchuk who was over six feet tall, and Danny for the obvious reason. The Christian names of some of the ones I mention above as well as some others are: George Glut, Theodore Matwijiw, George Dzundza, Steve Atamanchuck, William Rusnak, George Pasternak, Eugene Holowinsky and Eugene Tomashevsky. I mention their names to emphasize the point that some of their names sound Polish, yet their families came from western Galicia, and they considered themselves Ukrainians. We all went to St. George Church. We did not talk of being immigrants, nor did the Ukrainians among us speak Ukrainian because some of the boys were of Italian ancestry, but I assumed that a number of the ones I mention above had backgrounds similar to mine. Most of these boys were older than me by about a year or two, and ahead of me in both grade and high school, and I always compared myself with this reference group. We 'hung out' at the local soda fountain, played stick ball in the street and softball at a local park, pool and billiards, and a subset of these boys went to Coney Island in the summertime as a group. Only one boy had a car, and we went on car rides to the beach or to the Palisades Amusement Park in New Jersey, by contributing toward the purchase of gasoline, at 25 cents a gallon. We would sometimes entertain ourselves by going to night court, near City Hall, to see thieves, robbers, derelicts and prostitutes arraigned. I became best friends with George Dzundza (he was called Fatty) in my freshman year of high school. George had a similar background to mine: he arrived as an immigrant with only his mother, his father also having died in Germany. His mother was Polish but she spoke some Ukrainian and a little English and that is how I communicated with her. He also went to St. George School. George and I became friends while in eight grade and we continued our friendship throughout high school. He was the funny one in our crowd. He enrolled in Cardinal Hayes in the sophomore year and after graduation, entered St. Johns University and majored in Theatre Arts, eventually embarking on a successful career in acting. He played a major role in *The Deer Hunter*, in 1978, a movie about the Vietnam War, as well as one of the detectives in the TV series, *Law and Order* in the early 1990s. George was also a member of the Drum and Bugle corps (he played the drums), and Club 33. Georges mother was very kind to Dorothea and I; she bought us our TV set when we were married, and gave us a still life oil painting, the first picture for our new apartment.

Life on 12th Street and High School Years

Sometime in my freshman or sophomore year in high school we moved to 12th Street, between Avenues A and B, and this apartment was the last that I spent living with Mom and my brothers. We had been slowly transitioning to a traditional US household: we had a TV and a phone, I had a Ukrainian girlfriend, and a group of friends which provided my social group. I was 14 years old and a sophomore at Cardinal Hayes High School, and I met Dorothea when I turned 15, sometime in my sophomore year of high school. We got married out of this apartment. At this time, Wasyl was no longer living with us and only showed up occasionally to check up on Nick and John.

The apartment on 12th street is where I spent my formative teenage years, i.e. the sophomore, junior and senior years of high school. This apartment was on the edge of the Ukrainian community and there was a large difference in the ethnic composition of this block. The buildings were grittier, with beaten-up garbage cans and can covers strewn about in front of the buildings, vacant and boarded up storefronts. This was the time period of social unrest in the country, and when drugs permeated the neighborhood. Across the street from our building was a Puerto Rican men's club where on hot summer evenings open-shirted clad men would play dominoes on top of a makeshift table, and a radio would blare salsa music. There were also black families living on this block. We lived on the second floor in a four-room apartment, on the south side, facing the street. I'll mention one incident to illustrate my point of how rough this block was. I had a number of confrontations with Puerto Ricans going to-and-from 7th Street and one evening while I was on the phone with Dorothea, a shot was fired through the living room window. This was a bit disconcerting to say the least, and after this incident, my mom and I discussed moving closer to 7th Street. Dorothea and I got married in September of 1964 before my mom moved out of this apartment.

It was during this period that Tompkins Square Park became the center of a drug culture that was a hallmark of the beatnik culture and their lifestyle. Our neighborhood got the reputation of having readily available drugs and this perception drew outsiders to buy these drugs. As a young adolescent and teenager one needed to be careful not to get caught up in drugs, and surprisingly most of my friends did not use drugs. Neither our school nor the parents taught us about drugs, but it was understood that this was bad and we stayed away from the drug dealers. Unfortunately, my brother John got caught up in the drugs.

John and Nick moved with my mom to the 10th Street address and John continued to live with her after Dmytro and Nick got married. My mom went through a period of years when John drank and did drugs and this was very difficult for her. I was very angry with John and talked to my mom to throw him out of the house, but she wouldn't do it. She said if she threw him out he would wind up on the stoop at her apartment building and she would have to see him every time she went in and out of the building. John eventually kicked the habit, joined Narcotics Anonymous and spoke to groups around the neighborhood about the danger of drugs. After the Sept. 11, 2001 attacks on the World Trade Centers, he developed a lung infection and was put on narcotic drugs at the hospital. This led him again to addiction and he was found dead in 2003 in the apartment. The cause of death was listed as a heart attack but I suspected that it was a result of an overdose.

My mom continued to live on 12th Street until about 1966 when she moved to the apartment on 10th Street near Avenue A, on the 5th floor, and she walked up and down those stairs for approximately 40 years, the last of which she even carried her 40-pound dog, Bobek, up those stairs. She continued to live there until 1994 when she moved to a city project development on 4th street between 1st Avenue and Avenue A. This was a high-rise, studio apartment, on the 8th floor, in a building with an elevator. My mom died shortly after moving in.

High School Years and New Horizons

My graduation from 8th grade in 1959 and attending Cardinal Hayes High School were the beginnings of my leaving the neighborhood, the Ukrainian community, and in some sense escaping the chaos of the family. As I've already said, the idea of leaving or escaping is the general progression of immigrants who live in a ghetto. Ghetto life is a dead end for adults that do not assimilate; there is no future except for the hope of saving and scraping together money, and getting an education for their children so that they, the children, could get a job and help the parents with finances to relocate into other parts of the city or state. Everyone's aim was to leave the neighborhood, and many of the people had a good chance of accomplishing this goal. In my case, without a father in the house, it was especially difficult; I did not think we had this option open to us. As I've already mentioned, my Mom was co-habitating with Wasyl Bodnar but this co-habitation would not get us out of our situation, especially since Dmytro, Mary and I would not accept Wasyl as our family member. Our family was again stuck in a situation similar to that in Germany: the Ukrainians around us were leaving and we would be stuck at our location, perhaps the last to leave. A ghetto environment is also a dead end for the houses of worship since, as the immigrant generation ages and dies, and the young grow up and leave, the community dissolves. The clergy at St. George Parish was well aware of this and tried to come up with activities for young people, to tie them to the neighborhood so that, even if they moved away, they'd want to at least come back to worship on Sunday. This description of the progression of immigrants out of their communities as they become assimilated was what everyone was striving for but in our case this escape was hard to do.

My plan of leaving the neighborhood began with attending Cardinal Hayes High School. Cardinal Hayes was one of a number of all-boy Catholic schools in the city, subsidized by the Catholic Archdiocese. It had a good reputation for academics as did the other catholic schools such as Regis, Fordham Prep, and Xavier Academy. The decision to attend Cardinal Hayes was suggested by Sister Theodosia, one of my teachers, and I was happy to apply since I didn't want to attend the local public school which was known for gangs and for being dangerous, especially to boys. However, Catholic schools cost money and in this case, the subsidized tuition at Cardinal Hayes was $15/month. My mom paid the tuition in the freshman and sophomore years, and as I turned 15, and permitted to work, I paid the tuition for the junior and senior years through hourly jobs.

Cardinal Hayes was and still is a Catholic all-boys school in The Bronx with the main campus on the Grand Concourse (approximately 150th Street and the Grand Concourse). Cardinal Hayes had a large student body in the 1960s; there were approximately 2000 boys in the school at that time, with 581 boys in my graduating class in 1963. These Catholic high schools were well regarded in New York and a number of well know alums from Cardinal Hayes several years ahead of me include Regis Philbin and Martin

Scorsese. When I started there, the school had an oversubscription of freshman so the boys in Manhattan attended a building Annex located on 13th Street and 10th Avenue. Freshman would transition to the main campus in the Bronx for their last three years. The Annex was a large office-type building which was about a mile west of my home, near the Hudson River. Very few boys from the Ukrainian neighborhood attended Cardinal Hayes and I had to make friends with boys from the upper west side of Manhattan, and boys of other ethnic minorities. For example, I got to know a Polish boy by the name of Danilchuck and a boy from Columbia, SA who introduced me to eating fried pork skin (chicharon). The students were mainly Irish and Italian judging from the names of my 1963 Yearbook, and there were 18 black boys in my graduation class out of a class of 581. I mention the number of African-American boys because in 2019 the school is predominantly African-American and Hispanic.

This Annex in Manhattan was a six-story structure and I remember the wooden desks with attached seats, the slanted desktop, and wooden floor boards that creaked. The academic program was rigorous, with discipline instilled by Christian Brothers and I recall Brother Christopher as being the Principal during this time. Discipline involved strict rules of study and dress, and behavior. We wore jackets and ties and, when the report cards were handed out by Brother Christopher at the end of the period, you were called up in alphabetical order to the front of the room and either were congratulated for good grades or got a wallop in the face, with an open hand, for any grade lower than a B. I fit in and did well in freshman year, I never did get hit, but the next three years were a different story. I did not do well academically because of distractions by two organizations, and girls. My junior and senior years in high school were shaped by two organizations, sponsored by the St. George Church.

Drum Corp Years

It was in the period 1959-1960 that one of the priests, suggested that St. George Church start a drum and bugle corps, the Knights of St. George, to keep the boys and girls off the streets and encourage stronger ties of youngsters to the church and neighborhood. This was a brilliant strategic idea since it gave some of the teenagers a way to work off the rush of hormones, and a way for the adults to keep track of the them. The Knights of St. George Drum and Bugle Corp was mainly composed of Ukrainian boys and girls, with some Italian boys in the horn line and one African American boy in the drum line. The corps consisted of about 30 boys playing one-valved bugles, and 10 playing drums, and about 10 girls carrying an assortment of flags (the color guard). You were taught to read music, and play and march in formation.

The church purchased the uniforms and horns, drums and flags, and the boys were required to provide the mouthpieces for the horns, and their own drum sticks. The uniforms were made of short double-breasted jackets with tails and epaulets, and a rope garland around the right shoulder, with black pants with a black, one inch wide silk ribbon sewed on the side of the pant leg. We wore a stiff circular, high–hat shaped cap (shako), with a visor and a feather plume, which gave the appearance of a military uniform of the type you'd see in movies showing soldiers in the French army in the 1800's. The church hired the horn and drum instructors, and the boys learned to read and play music while marching and maneuvering. This was supposed to be a self-sustaining enterprise. The horn instructor, George Rodrigues, was a middle-aged man who had fought in WWII and was a very good soprano horn player. He knew the music of the 30's, 40's and 50's and this is what he taught us. We got to know pop songs from these early decades-Frank Sinatra ballads, songs from *West Side Story*, jazz tunes of Duke Ellington, and music of operas such as Bizet's *Carmen*. A wide and interesting variety that has shaped my taste in music ever since.

The funding for this organization was a mixture of fund raising, getting hired by business organizations to play at parades such as at the St. Patrick's Day parade in Manhattan, and church donations. Adults supervised and organized these activities. The boys and girls spent one or two evenings a week memorizing and practicing songs, and marching routines. Besides the drum corps activities, many of the boys and girls paired off as boyfriend and girlfriend.

The Knights of St. George was a very important for me since it channeled my efforts into a structured organization, taught me the rudiments of music, and kept me disciplined. It was through the corps that I eventually met Dorothea. I will describe how this happened in a subsequent section.

Part 3

My High School Years

Attending Cardinal Hayes High School shaped my life by initially teaching me discipline. At the time that I was in the Drum and Bugle Corps, I attended the Annex, and in the sophomore year, I transitioned to the Bronx campus on the Grand Concourse. Getting there took a long subway ride of approximately 45 minutes. The dress code was a white shirt and navy blue tie, a navy jacket and black leather shoes. I was again conditioned to wear a 'uniform.' Some planning was needed to get to school on time since assembly was at 8am and there were consequences for being late. The boys living in Manhattan or Brooklyn needed to arrive well before assembly, and time the short walk from the subway stop to the Cardinal Hayes building, a matter of several blocks, to make it to the front doors on time. More time was needed for those of us that smoked cigarettes and this was done as we hung around the exit of the subway since we were strictly forbidden to smoke anywhere near the school. To give an example of the strict discipline at Cardinal Hayes, the Principal, Father Jablonski at the time, would sometimes walk over to the subway stop to see if boys were smoking or, inspect the haircuts of the boys as they exited the subway stop, to see if their hair fell below their shirt collar.

I was not a particularly good student in high school but I had interest in Physics and Chemistry, and also in History and

English. One of my teachers encouraged us to read the New York Times which I have continued to do throughout my life in spite of the fact that my political opinions have begun to differ from the Editorial pages over the years. When I was 15, I also enjoyed reading about national politics, was a fan of John Kennedy and Barry Goldwater, and watched every political presidential convention since 1960. I took Latin as my language requirement the first two years and Spanish the last two, and I memorized Shakespearean sonnets and soliloquies as part of lessons in English literature, and I still have some of the books that we were required to read. I registered and took a course in self-learning calculus but I disliked the self-learning style.

My Sophomore, Junior and Senior years in high school were filled with going to and from school, 'hanging out' with boys and girls in the neighborhood, learning how to play a baritone bugle, and marching and maneuvering in the Drum corps. When you are a teenager, time seems to stand still; there is plenty of time to do homework, chores at home, catch up with your friends, talk to girls. These are the excuses I now give for not being very good academically in my sophomore, junior and senior years. A cadre of us teenage boys continued to hang out around 7th Street, and we typically tried to find ways to amuse ourselves by playing stickball, soccer, softball, or singing pop songs.

We were not hooligans, but the adults wanted to channel our restlessness so that we wouldn't get into trouble. One of the priests, Father Patrick, suggested that the boys that were not interested in the Drum and Bugle Corps, form a social 'club,' and locate ourselves at a building owned by the church at 33 East 7th Street, on the fourth floor, where we would pay a nominal rent. This was to be an all-boys club with home base in, at-the-time, vacant building. I assume that our presence provided some form of protection for the building from vandalism. This, of course, was another brilliant move by the Parish because this allowed the adults to know where the teenagers that were not in the drum and bugle corps were in the evenings and to control, to some extent, what we did. I became one of the founding members. We compiled Bylaws, collected membership fees, and designed rules where each boy was to wear on special occasions, such as a dark navy jacket with the club emblem-Club 33-affixed to the chest pocket. The Club also sponsored weekend dances in the basement of the building, where the club members and other teenagers in the neighborhood brought their dates, drank beer and alcohol, danced to 'doo wop' songs and smooched in the hallways on a Saturday evening. Dorothea and I attended a number of these dances and we became an item, everyone recognizing that we were a couple. The Club charged admission to the dances and even though we were all under the age of drinking, had a cash bar, the money used to pay for the rent.

So, there were two things going on during this time: Club 33, which occupied the fourth floor of the building at 33 E. 7th Street, was formed, a subset of the boys joined the Knights of St. George Drum and Bugle Corps, and all the teenagers were going to various high schools. It was during this time, when I was 14 and 15 years old, that my break with the local community began in earnest, partly as a result of my high school experiences, and the disbanding of the Knights of St. George.

Another lucky break

You never know where the fork in the road will show up, where you will make a decision that will follow you for the rest of your life. In my case, after about a year or so of membership in the Knights of St. George Drum and Bugle Corps, the drum corps disbanded because of lack of resources and I was given an opportunity to further explore the world outside my neighborhood. I don't know why this venture outside of the neighborhood stands out to me more than going to Cardinal Hayes, but it certainly opened my eyes to what was possible and presented opportunities beyond what I had experienced so far. George Rodriguez, the horn instructor of the Knights of St. George, asked a number of the boys to consider joining the Floyd Bennett Golden Eagles, a corps in Brooklyn which he also had been instructing. The Golden Eagles were sponsored by the American Legion Post #1060 located on Avenue N and 56th Street in Flatbush, Brooklyn and at first I was undecided about joining because it was at least an hour away by subway and bus from my home in Manhattan. The ride included an IRT subway ride to the Brooklyn Bridge or South Ferry station and then catching the express IRT train, with the last stop being at Flatbush Ave. The final leg of this trip was to catch the Flatbush Avenue bus to 56th Street. This was a journey of about an hour, with several delays between catching the next train, and usually with a wait for the bus. This location in Mill Basin, Brooklyn was a far-off outpost of New York. The tree-lined streets were wide, and the two or three-story tall buildings on Flatbush Avenue had business establishments, as had Avenue N. The local streets on either side of Avenue N had duplexes (semi-attached homes), and every now and one could see a dirt footpath in the middle of the blocks separating Avenue N and Avenue M. I was told that some of the homes even had goats. The boys from Manhattan considered this the backwater of NY. I had a hard time imagining that I'd stick with this drum corps. In spite of our biased views of this part of Brooklyn, several of us from St. George decided to give the Golden Eagles a try and it was here that I met a whole new set of teenaged boys and girls, not immigrants, developed my horn-playing skills and began dating Dorothea.

The Golden Eagles were a much better corps than the Knights of St. George; their horn line and drumline was better, their marching and maneuvering was better, and they were plugged into contests with corps from around Long Island, New Jersey and the northeast part of the US. These Drum Corps competitions involved a playing and marching routine of the type you see at halftime at college football games. The horn line practiced at the American Legion Post, and the marching and maneuvering at the Floyd Bennett airfield in Brooklyn. The marching at parades was seen as a way of making money to sustain the group, and secondary to the contests. We competed with corps from around the northeast and hoped to 'graduate' from these junior corps to that of senior units with membership for ages over 18. This was all new to me, would expand my horizons, and I liked the challenge and was determined to stick it out with them. This was not so with the other boys from Manhattan. Most of them dropped out within the first few months and I was one of two or three that stayed.

The remaining few got integrated into the Floyd Bennett social structure, being invited to parties, and meeting and dating the girls of the Golden Eagles. This is where I was introduced to Dorothea and began dating her several months after my joining the corps. We Manhattanites also introduced the Brooklynites to Manhattan, inviting them to the Club 33 parties and helping them explore the lower east side. My time was now spent juggling drum corps practices, high school studies, dating Dorothea, and Club 33.

Work Experience During High School and After Graduation

I had always expected to work but was not allowed to until I got my work permit when I turned 15. At that time, I got a job as a delivery boy at a Pharmacy, then as a soda jerk, all the time looking to get higher pay. The job minimum pay at that time was one dollar per hour. Jobs were hard to come by, but I eventually obtained a job, in my junior year of high school, as a mail clerk in the Wall Street area of downtown Manhattan, on 102 Maiden Lane, at an agency that sold life insurance. My hours were from after school, i.e. after the train ride from the Bronx, until 5pm. The Clark Agency sold life insurance policies of the Connecticut Mutual Life Insurance Company, and it was located on the eleventh floor, overlooking the South Street Seaport. It was a typical small company with perhaps 10 agents and ten secretaries sitting in cubicles in a large open space in the center of the room and I was the only mail clerk situated in a small separate room which I also used for my work as well as my desk. I collected letters and packages containing policies from the agent's desks, placed stamps on this mail and deposited it downstairs in the mail box between the elevators of the building or carried the packages to a post office location. I made trips to other insurance firms in uptown Manhattan, and kept the copier serviced. I hated taking care of the copier which used the liquid, Thermofax process, the precursor of the Xerox dry copier process. This copier was about the size of a typical fax/copier machine you may be familiar with, about 12x12x8 inches. The care of the copier involved dumping the liquid in the toilet of the bathroom, washing out the tray that contained the liquid and cleaning the rollers. This was a messy and smelly job and it was the worse job in the entire firm.

    I worked for the Clark Agency until I graduated from high school in 1963, right up to the time I enrolled in Bronx Community College that Fall. One of my saddest memories of these years was hearing of the assassination of President John Kennedy on November 22, 1963, near the end of my tenure of work there.

Pre-Marriage

I worked five days a week, after school, and on Tuesday evening I travelled to Flatbush for horn practice from 6 to 9pm, spent time with Dorothea when I could, then returned home by 11pm.

Figure 34. A photobooth photo of Dorothea and I sometime in 1962. I'm not sure of the location.

Dorothea tells the story that the first time she saw me, when we Manhattanites arrived at the American Legion Post to be introduced to the Golden Eagles, she knew we would be married and spend our lives together. I don't remember her at this first visit and it took some time for us to be introduced at a party at the home of one of her friends. She was, and still is, beautiful, with a cute upturned nose, but looked young, too young for me, when we met. It was only later that I learned she was only three months younger than I. I was smitten by her good looks and figure, and of course her personality. Ours was a 'long-distance' relationship, but despite this inconvenience, we fell in love and would see each other at drum corps practice and usually have a date on the weekend. I'd make the extra trip to Brooklyn at least once a week. In addition to the Drum corps practice, Club 33 would sometimes hold a dance party on a Saturday night, and Dorothea would travel to Manhattan, and I would take her home in the evening. Only a teenager would have the energy to do this. We met while we were Juniors in high school and dated until we graduated from high school in June 1963. My graduation ceremony was in St. Patrick's Cathedral in midtown Manhattan and Dorothea's at Tilden High School in Brooklyn, but we did not attend each other's ceremonies.

Turmoil and Excitement is how I would describe the years 1963 and 1964. My family had two young children aged 5 and 6 at this time, and it was the job of everyone to contribute to their care. Dmytro and I played with John and Nick, took them to Tomkins Square Park and East River Park, fed them when necessary, and generally helped out in their care. Dorothea also had two young children in her family, Lori and Billy, born in 1959 and 1961 respectively. She also had the responsibility of helping in their care, and as you'd expect with teenagers, we commiserated that this infringed on our time together. Little did we know the turmoil that would sweep us up in the next two years.

In the 1960s, it was assumed that as young people graduated high school, the boys would work in a profession such as machinist, policeman, bus driver, or teacher, and the girls would get married and stay home to take care of any children. Only a small fraction of high school graduates went to college. This was the norm, and initially I expected this type of life for myself. However, Dorothea and I came to have other ambitions. The idea of college came into my mind because I thought college would be a way to elevate myself beyond what was expected of me, while Dorothea had always talked of becoming a nurse. This was the beginnings of a plan that we both bought into. However, life never turns out the way you initially think. I was not admitted to my first choice of college, The City College, but was offered a scholarship to attend any number of other community colleges in New York. Community colleges were meant to be a feeder schools for The City College and it was guaranteed that if you can graduate from one of these two-year schools, then you would automatically be admitted to The City College. Bronx Community College was the school I chose because it was located in The Bronx, at 183rd Street, and I was used to travelling there, the area was familiar to me. In the meantime, Dorothea received a scholarship to attend Nursing School. I continued to work at the Clark Agency and registered to attend Bronx Community College for Fall 1963. Part of the requirements of receiving the scholarship was that I apply for citizenship as soon as I turned 18 (in December 1963), and I applied and was naturalized on May 4, 1965. I include a picture of my naturalization certificate in Figure 35 below.

Figure 35. My Naturalization Certificate. I am now 20 lbs heavier than the weight quoted in this document.

During this time, Dorothea and I were love-struck and talked on the phone constantly. That summer, without our parent's knowledge, we talked about marriage and it was that Fall that I spotted an engagement ring in the window of a jewelry shop across the street from where I worked and started a lay-away plan to buy it. At this time, I had been at Bronx Community college for one year, the fall of 1963 and spring of 1964, and was planning the transition to The City College. I was also waiting for my draft classification.

In the Spring of 1964, Dorothea left nursing school, and got a job as a clerk in Manhattan at a steamship company, and, our wedding plans accelerated when, that summer, we found out that Dorothea was pregnant. I immediately put my plans of college for the fall of 1964 on hold and got a job with United Parcel Service as a truck helper. We were married in September of that year and little did I know that I would be laid off the day before the marriage.

Marriage

Our marriage got off to a rocky start; we were 18 years old, Dorothea was pregnant with Christine, and I lost my job with United Parcel Service the day before our wedding. Marriages are not supposed to last under these circumstances. Being so young, who knows how we would develop, perhaps grow apart. Would we be able to stand the stress of having a young child? Could we make ends meet with perhaps my only being able to get a menial job? Luckily it all worked out; we were happy and optimistic because our family and friends closed ranks and supported us, and we were in love and resilient. We managed to stay married these 55-plus years because of our love, and the flexibility to adapt and accommodate each other.

Dorothea and I were married in St. George Church on September 19, 1964 in a traditional ceremony, with George Dzundza as best man and Dorothea's sister Lee, as matron of honor. This was a traditional Ukrainian wedding where the bride and groom walk down the aisle, with the best man and matron of honor holding a crown of flowers above our heads. In our case, the priest blessed our path with incense, and wedding prayers were sung in Church Slovanic. We didn't know the meaning of these words, and to this day, we joke, we don't know if we were asked the question 'do you take this man/woman to be your lawfully wedded husband/wife.'

The wedding party and guests then loaded up into several cars and headed for the reception at the Dorothea's family home with aunts, uncles, and friends, of both our families. Dorothea's father filmed the reception using his 8mm movie camera, with floodlights spread on a rack that looked like deer antlers. One of my memories of the reception was my friends dancing the 'hopak,' a traditional Ukrainian dance in the living room. After this reception Dorothea's dad, with Lee, drove us to our apartment, where we sat on the empty living room floor and had a champagne toast.

Figure 36. Photo showing the three generations of females at the day of our wedding and reception at Dorothea's family home. Shown are Dorothea and I, my mom, Dorothea's maternal grandmother, Elizabeth, and Dorothea's mother, Dorothea, but called Thea. Note the sassy pose of my mom.

I will now backtrack a little to describe the events leading up to our marriage. As I have said above, prior to our wedding, in June of 1964, Dorothea began a job as a clerk at a steamship company (the States Marine Isthmian Line), in lower Manhattan, while in July, I started full-time but temporary work at the United Parcel Service as an 'apprentice' (a trucker's helper) in the garment district of Manhattan. I was the labor that worked with a driver, picking up packages in the garment district in Manhattan, loading them on a panel truck and taking the packages to the main UPS facility on the west side of 42nd street. Mine was a temporary job, for a period of approximately two months, under arrangement with the Teamsters Union, that included all the workers at United Parcel. It was the Union's prerogative to accept or reject apprentices, so that new hires did not displace existing union workers. So, it was difficult to get a permanent job unless a union member retired or otherwise left the company. I very much wanted this job and Union membership since it was known that the pay, job security and benefits were very good. Dorothea and I were confident that we could make ends meet with our two jobs but after two months on the job I received notice, the Friday before our wedding, that I was being laid off. Dorothea's was then our only income and that weekend I got busy looking through ads in the New York papers for a job.

While we were preparing for marriage, we signed a two-year lease on a small, three room, railroad-flat basement apartment of a single-story home on East 53rd Street and Avenue N, just three blocks from the Rumstich residence. I mention the two-year lease because a year after we moved in the landlord wanted to re-take possession of the apartment for his own family, and we would have to find another place to live when the lease expired. This transition of moving complicated our lives since we had made a decision, near the end of 1966, to move to Delaware for the Spring semester at the University of Delaware in January 1967. In the summer of 1966 we ended up living in the basement of Dorothea's parent's home for approximately the four-month period.

I have fond memories of the apartment on 53rd Street. It is out of this apartment, from November 1964 to December 1966, that I again took a job with United Parcel Service and met Herbie Young (which I will describe shortly), and started work for Joan Toggitt in the period of January 1965 to the Fall of 1966. What I found interesting about this apartment was that each of the three rooms, except for the bathroom, had a window, at eye level of Mill Lane, a dirt path, which was used by Dorothea and Lee, to walk to their grade school, P.S. 203. I felt that I was in a better position from where I came; this was new construction in a stand-alone house, with no roaches or rodents, newly painted, and with a shower with working fixtures.

The day after the wedding reception, I scoured the newspapers for job openings and made note of three possibilities; as a Fuller Brush salesman (my job would be to visit potential customers in lower Manhattan to convince them to buy products such as combs, brushes and the like, so I did not accept the job), a draftsman job at an architectural firm (I didn't have experience), and that of an R&D technician. I called about the R&D position and recall sitting at a desk of the interviewer who asked me if I had any experience in R&D. I told her that I didn't know what R&D was and she replied that this meant that I didn't meet the criteria for the job and abruptly ended the interview. As I was leaving I turned around and asked what R&D stood for and she refused to tell me. So don't you be discouraged with disappointments.

I was unemployed for several weeks until I reapplied at UPS as a seasonal worker for the Christmas season of 1964 (for a ten-week period until December 24th) after which, it was understood that I'd be laid off again. I was assigned to a storefront location on 34th street and 8th Avenue, my job being to stack and sort packages in the back room, and sometimes to assist the driver in deliveries. I was very discouraged at this time especially since there were many boys and young men doing this same job as holiday work between semesters of well-known colleges. I remember comments being made by the union men about these college students; jokes as to how they would go back to their presumably rich lifestyles or suburban homes, the football teams they played on and the fraternities they belonged to. I was envious that I didn't have this in my future.

While working at UPS, I met an African-American young man, Herbie Young, about my age, who also worked as a Truckers helper and he had gotten laid off from UPS just as I, and as we went our separate ways, he and I both promised we'd keep each other in mind if a job came up. He quickly got a job with a small company in Manhattan and he offered to introduce me to the owner of a small mail-order company, Joan Toggitt Ltd., that imported wool and embroidery kits. Joan Toggitt Ltd. was founded and owned by Mrs. Joan Toggitt; I interviewed with her and began as the shipping clerk and office helper at 34th Street and Vanderbilt Avenue in Manhattan, adjacent to Grand Central Station. Mrs. Toggitt influenced my life and was a big help to Dorothea and I as we were settling into our marriage. I mention Herbie not only because he introduced me to Mrs. T but because we shared a bond of having uncertain futures; he was newly married with a daughter on the way later that year, and he was raised in a working- class family in Harlem. Our friendship went on for several years during which we invited each other to our homes and Dorothea and I met his family and friends. You can perhaps imagine how unusual it was to be the only white couple at a party at his home, and vice versa, when he and his family came to our apartment on 53rd Street.

Christine was born in March of 1965, in Interborough General Hospital, a small community hospital on Linden Boulevard in Brooklyn, at the end of an evening when we were babysitting Billy and Lori, while Dorothea's parents were at a formal dinner dance. Dorothea went into labor during the evening and we called her doctor and met him at his office for determination as to how things were progressing. He confirmed that Dorothea was ready for delivery and told us to go to the hospital and check in after midnight so that we would not be charged for an additional day. Dorothea's mother, in a sequined gown, and her father, in a tuxedo, left their affair before coffee was served, and arrived home in time for Dorothea's mother to drive us to the hospital, running every red light. Going through childbirth in 1964, was very different from what you are familiar with. In our case, on registering at the front desk after midnight, a nurse took Dorothea to a 'holding area,' and Dorothea's mother and I were left sitting in a dimly-lit waiting room, waiting for the doctor to show up. Dorothea's mother left after some time and I called Herbie, who drove me to his home to pass the time. When I was driven back at the hospital, I continued waiting and never saw the doctor come in. Christine was born at 5:30 am and I only learned of Christine's birth by inadvertently seeing the doctor leaving, and yelling after him. He was surprised by my yell but then returned to say that Dorothea was fine and that the baby was a girl. I only came to see Christine through the window of the nursery, went home and returned later that day. We brought beautiful, baby Christine home after three days.

Looking back at the two and a half years from June 1964 to the Fall of 1966, it seems as if there was one crisis after another. There was the death of my Babcha and Dorothea's grandparents, Dorothea's mom serious illness, and her Dad losing his job at Sperry. As I've already described, our lease ran out that summer of 1966, and we waited to move to Delaware. How our marriage survived these two years is a miracle, and I chalk it up to our love and the support we received from our families.

More on My Environment in the 1960s

Although I've already written about some of the political and cultural changes going on the 1960's, I'll describe some more details of my environment in the 1960's since this outside environment played a big role in my maturing as an individual and as a husband and father. So far, I have written about my boyhood in the 1950's and as the 60's rolled around I entered high school and started wandering outside the neighborhood. I came to realize how quickly life was changing from that of 1950-1960. For example, I became aware of the mayoral and presidential elections, racial issues in the city and country, and what we lately have come to call culture wars. The culture wars of today (2019) and the political turmoil are nothing compared to what was going on in the 1960's. If you read some history of that time period (see for example; *The Global Age* by Kershaw), you'll recognize that there were big political and cultural changes sweeping across the US in the 1960s; rock and roll music was replacing the '40's big band sounds; Elvis, the Beatles and Bob Dylan represented this transition in music, and teenagers were beginning, at an accelerated pace, to discard the morals and traditions of their elders. The cold war was in full swing, and the Vietnam war was heating up. War protests, and the civil rights of African-Americans were some of the major issues in the country; there were race riots in New York City in the summer of 1964. Of course, the Kennedy and King assassinations shocked us all. Mohammed Ali, the pill, women's lib, the list could go on and on.

The one global event that impacted me directly was the war in Vietnam. I was slated to be called up for military service as soon as I turned 18. I was at the top of the list to be classified as 1A, for getting drafted into the US army. The Selective Service and Training Act issued in 1940, as the first peacetime draft, required that eligible men be conscripted. However, in 1963, there were exemptions for those who were in school or were married. The draft notice I received just after I turned 18, near the end of 1964, after our marriage, had me listed as 3A, so that I would not be the first drafted. As the war expanded, the draft rules were changed in August 1965 by President Johnson, so that being in school, or married with a child, no longer exempted young men from the draft. I continued to be classified as 3A and was not subject to being called into service. At the wars' peak, this led to the burning of draft cards and flight of young men to Canada. By the luck of the draw I escaped being called up, but many of my high school friends were drafted, sent to Vietnam, and died there.

The Joan Toggitt Period

I was hired by Mrs. Toggitt, to work in her small, mail-order company in Manhattan mailing of packages and tidying the showroom, during the period after I was laid off from UPS, in approximately January 1965. Joan Toggitt was an emigre Austrian Jew that had escaped Austria in the early stages of WWII by emigrating to Shanghai. She had told me that her husband had died sometime during the war and she made her way to Shanghai since this was one of the few 'free' cities, as she put it, that would accept immigrants without passport documents. While in Shanghai, she started a company that manufactured knitted sweaters and, she was very proud of the fact that she taught young Chinese girls to knit, using wool she imported from Scotland. She always called them 'her girls.' After the war and after the passage of the Amendment to the Displaced Persons Act of 1948 which allowed for 4,000 immigrants that had escaped Europe to the Orient to be accepted into the US, she applied for emigration, was successfully processed and started an importing company in New York City. Who could have imagined that an immigrant would have provided a lifeline to Dorothea and me. She was perhaps 50 years old when I met her, with long, peppered-gray hair that she usually wore in a bun at the back of her head, and glasses with circular rims. Mrs. Toggitt was a diminutive woman that had had polio as a young girl and developed a partially-atrophied left leg, and a hunchback. When she walked, she purposely, and with exaggeration, lifted her left leg before putting it down. She usually used a cane and wore black or polka-dotted dresses, and spoke with an Austrian/German accent. Despite this look of a handicapped woman she was an imposing personality that gave you the feeling that she had vast experience and knowledge and sophistication, and could take care of herself.

Figure 37. Photo of Dorothea and Mrs. Toggitt, in Mrs. T's apartment (early 1965).

I started working for Mrs. Toggitt in 1965, at 42 Vanderbilt Ave, the building located between 34th and 36th Streets, on the west side of Grand Central Station. The company occupied two small offices on the 13th floor, with windows overlooking the

My Fortunate Immigrant Life

Grand Central Station. The company survived through advertisements in craft magazines that sold embroidery kits and supplies and books to retail customers. One of the offices was used as the showroom where examples of embroidery kits, books and skeins of wool were displayed in cabinets and on shelves. The second office had three rooms, a larger one where kits were prepared, a room that contained a desk used by a part-time book keeper, and two smaller rooms, one serving as the office for Mrs. T, and a mail room. My job was to keep the showroom tidy, and to prepare packages of skeins of wool, books and embroidery kits into boxes, affixed the postage label and postage, and carry the packages to the post office. I would sometimes be asked to pick up lunch for those in the office from a local restaurant; she always ordered an egg salad sandwich on white bread, and a cup of hot tea. Mrs. Toggitt also hired unemployed, aspiring actresses at those months in the summer, when the fall acting season was in preparation. I was intrigued with meeting these aspiring actresses and hearing about their New York experiences in search of opportunities. I, on the other hand, wanted to leave New York as soon as possible.

Mrs. T and I liked each other from the first time we met, and she took on a benefactress-type of role with Dorothea and me. She tried to teach me a more sophisticated life; knowledge that I hadn't receive at home. For example, she talked to me about saving some of my salary and personally walked me to a bank to start an account for Christine. She made an appointment for me to see a dentist and, one day, she took Dorothea and I to a formal lunch at a fancy restaurant and showed me/us how to order our meal, and wine at lunch. On this day, Mrs. Toggitt ordered the wine and when the waiter arrived with the bottle, he opened it and poured a small amount into my glass, since I was the man at the table. He waited for me to taste it and approve acceptance of the bottle. I didn't know this was how this was done and I just sat there without a thought as to why he kept standing next to me without filling everyone's glass. Finally, Mrs. T tapped me on the arm and told me discretely to taste the wine. I was embarrassed but learned a lesson I have since not forgotten.

Another incident bonded Mrs. T and myself. NYC went through a power blackout on Nov.9, 1965, near the evening rush hour, and as the building went dark and night started to descend on the city, we became concerned about how we would get to our homes. Of course, we needed to get to the street level and this was going to be difficult for Mrs. T. I carried her down the 13 flights of stairs and walked her to her apartment. I spent that evening with my mom at the 12th Street apartment, having walked there in the dark. It was eerie walking along dark streets where every so often ordinary citizens, with flashlights, would serve as traffic guards, stopping traffic to allow people to cross the intersection. The next day I walked to work and got home to Brooklyn at the end of the day by sharing a taxi with some strangers.

Mrs. T was disappointed when I turned her down for a full-time job at the firm. She tried to convince me that I could rise in the company and take over from her, but I had already planned my future and was surprised with her offer. I continued to work for Mrs. T until the fall of 1966 when I transferred to City College of New York. It was at this time that I was very anxious and went through panic attacks. I only got through this period by talking with Frank Moon.

The Rumstich Family

When Dorothea and I started on the path to marriage I had no idea of the extent of my bonding to her family. She had an interactive family with maternal grandparents, aunts and uncles, and cousins, all of whom visited and kept in touch with each other. Dorothea's family had a home and car, and I hoped to learn from this family as to how I could achieve this dream. The Rumstich family were German-Americans, and lived in the home initially bought by her maternal grandfather and grandmother, Oma and Opa Hoer, who emigrated to the US in 1927 between the two world wars. Opa Hoer was an engineer that worked on gyroscopes on ships and we have several photos of him displaying a new gyroscope he participated in designing and building for the Cunard line. At the time I met him and Dorothea's parents, Oma and Opa Hoer had retired to Florida and Dorothea's parents owned the house. The house was a semi-attached building on East 56th Street in the Flatbush area of Brooklyn with its mirror twin occupied by another family. Dorothea's father, William Rumstich, was 50 years old when I first met him in 1963. He was an Engraver by profession and a machinist at Sperry-Rand Corporation, working at the Lake Success location on Long Island. He was proud of his profession and told me how he was tasked to work on experimental technologies such as the production of travelling wave tubes for radar equipment and guidance systems for rocket propulsion. He taught me to operate the machinery in his shop, in the basement of his home, during the time Dorothea and I were dating. Bill Rumstich taught me how to use the lathe and drill press, sharpen tool bits and save every screw or nail you may ever find or buy. He also taught me how to drive his stick-shift car. I liked him but as is the case with most teenagers, when I first met him, I considered him to be out of touch with the special knowledge that I thought I had. I looked on him as Archie Bunker as portrayed in the 1960's sitcom and I suppose he thought of me as Meathead. He must have been puzzled when in answer to his question one afternoon as to what I wanted to do as a profession, I answered that I intended to be an electrical engineer. I think he was skeptical.

Dorothea's older sister, Lee, married Francis Moon in August 1962 and as I got to know Frank, he began to be a big influence in my life. Soon after we met, I recall him asking me what I wanted to do with my education. As I told him I liked math he commented matter-of-factly that I should consider being an engineer. I took this comment to heart and from that time considered myself pursuing an engineering degree. I eventually came to see Frank as a role model.

Frank and Lee Moon

Frank received his PhD in the summer of 1966 from Cornell University and accepted an assistant professorship in the Mechanical Engineering Department at the University of Delaware. I did not know much about colleges or universities outside of New York so my intent was on getting a BSEE degree in New York City. Frank recognized the long slog ahead, getting this degree by attending classes part-time and he counseled that moving out of the city would provide less distraction and allow me to finish my degree within a reasonable time. It was during the summer or fall of 1966 that he and Lee offered to support Dorothea and I during the school year, to attend the University of Delaware and that our obligation was to reciprocate by supporting another person after I got my degree. This offer of support was another of those events of good fortune that changed my life. We took them up on their offer and moved to Newark, Delaware in the Fall of 1966 where I started as an undergraduate electrical engineering student. I began classes that next Spring semester of 1967.

Frank and Lee Moon are an extraordinary couple that supported Dorothea and me at one of the crucial points in our lives. They invested in us but, as important, Frank provided the guidance and roll model to me. If he could do it then maybe I could also.

On the Road to Academia

Dorothea and I moved to Newark Delaware in the Fall of 1966. Newark (pronounced Nu Ark, the Ark sounded as in the Noah's Ark), Delaware was a small college town about fifteen miles southwest of Wilmington Delaware. It's a college town with the University of Delaware as a major employer. The town sits just south of the Mason-Dixon line in an area also dominated by the DuPont de Nemours Company, with small facilities scattered over the surrounding area. You may be interested to know that in prior centuries, the DuPont company manufactured dynamite and ammunition so the sites of manufacture were small separated buildings with three walls built of brick, instead of a large manufacturing facility. If an explosion occurred the non-brick side would blow out and small buildings would limit the damage of the explosion. At the time we arrived, UD had about 4,000 students, with a large Nursing Department and a small engineering college; there were approximately 23 students in Electrical Engineering in my graduating class of 1969.

Sometimes it's better not to know what you are getting yourself into as in our case when we moved to Delaware. We took it on faith that we'd survive on student loans, a potential or possible job at the university or town, and the stipend from the Moon's, but our calculations, no matter how we figured it, showed that this would be impossible. We moved anyway. We did not own a car. Our transportation was a used men's bicycle and a wicker child's seat that sat on the crossbar, bequeathed to us by Frank Moon, and we survived those two years on frugal living, various part-time jobs that I obtained and scholarships from the University, and clinging to the Moons, at least that first year. I got a job that first semester (Spring 1967) in the university video recording studio, helping with antenna installation on university buildings, and fixing electronic taping equipment. I also received a small scholarship from the Department, several hundred dollars for that same semester, and in the summer of 1967, I worked second shift (4-11pm) at National Vulcanized Fiber (NVF) Company, a spin-off of the Hercules Company, affixing casters on the bottoms of barrels made of vulcanized fiber, and sometimes being put on detail to load these huge barrels into railroad cars for transport to customers. These small jobs, especially in the summer months when we were without the Moon's stipend, and student loans from the Department of Defense helped us survive. As an aside, NVF produced pressed parts for use in railroads and other industries from cardboard and fabric, recycling these materials by placing them into huge vats filled with caustic chemicals that broke down the cellulose fiber, then pressing the cellulose into component parts after the chemicals were squeezed out. The heat and stench of the factory floor was overwhelming since the factory floor was not air conditioned nor the vapors ventilated. If you've ever been to the Chesapeake Bay area or Washington D.C. in the summer you'd appreciate my comments about the air conditioning. Loading the barrels into the boxcar was daunting; you don't know how big a boxcar is until you have to fill it with five-foot tall, four feet diameter barrels, four high.

The week that we arrived and settled in to our new home, the

Moon's informed us that they would be moving to Princeton University, that summer of 1967. I started my first semester at UD in the Spring semester, i.e. in January of 1967, and it was a potential disaster because of a senior level course in Electrical Machine Design. This senior level class was meant to fill in my schedule for full time attendance, but I did not have the prerequisites nor did I know that the teacher was a boring, uninteresting professor. There was a lot of pressure on me not to fail this course, but I somehow got through this class. As the semester wore on, I was befriended by several faculty, who gave me a part time jobs and Dorothea contributed to our finances by babysitting. My thinking at the time was to plod ahead, graduate, and hope for a good job as an engineer. The following year, I decided to get an advanced degree and decided to apply to Cornell University partly because I knew Frank had gone there and partly from recognizing names of faculty who were authors of technical papers I had read.

I did well in my classes at the University of Delaware, got inducted into two Engineering Honor Societies and I supplemented my classes with Physics and Philosophy. My interest in Physics came from reading Richard Feynman's books which I received as a Christmas gift from Dorothea in 1965. Feynman made the case that advances in the solid state were going to be important so I thought I could merge my interest in solid state electronics with electrical engineering. I applied to the newly formed Materials Science Department at Cornell and was accepted as a graduate student to work with Professor Che-Yu Li, in January 1969. I changed advisors after approximately one year of study and became the student of Jack Blakely. I opted out of doing a Masters degree and went on to the PhD. I had my PhD thesis accepted in the Spring semester of 1973.

Figure 38. Medallion of the Knights of St. George Drum and Bugle Corp, designed and fabricated by someone unknown to me.

Some Interesting Anecdotes while in Newark, Delaware

Figure 39. Photo of the back of 315 Ashley Road in Newark Delaware where we lived in 1967 and 1968. That's Christine standing in the yard. The large back yard ended with a railroad track on which the body of Robert Kennedy was taken to Washington, D.C..

Figure 40. Dorothea (pregnant with Kathryn) and Christine standing on the front steps of our home on Ashley Road, Newark, DE, c. 1968.

At the time we lived in Newark, our home, which was approximately a half mile from Main Street, was on the southern border of the University. It was approximately 600 square feet in area on the ground floor, with four rooms at street level and a musty, smelly basement. The front door let you into the living room with the kitchen to the right and two small bedrooms at the back of the house that faced a large back yard that ended at the railroad tracks of the Pennsylvania Rail Road. It was this rail line which carried the body of Robert Kennedy on June 8, 1968, from St. Patrick's Cathedral, to where he was buried at Arlington National Cemetery, and by which we, along with some of our neighbors, stood by with hands on our hearts in his honor.

There was a factory a few blocks from our house (owned by the Hercules Company, a subsidiary of the DuPont Company) and several of the days of the week, a light mist of chemicals fell on our house, saturating the ground and us if we were outdoors. By the way, when we visited Newark in 2019 this factory was gone, replaced by Townhomes. Thinking back on our time in Newark, we were there a mere two years, we continued to have strong relationships with our two families and had many visitors, including Dorothea's parents, Lori and Billy, Mary, and my brothers. For example, John (age 13) and Nick (age 12) and Billy (age 10) were sent to stay with us for several weeks in the summer of 1968.

Newark is a suburban-type town, there was no public transportation, so, without a car, we either walked to town or were driven by neighbors or friends. I don't know how Dorothea managed pulling a two-wheeler cart from our home to Main street, with Christine in tow, to wash cloth diapers. We visited the usual sights, when we could get a ride, such as to Rehoboth Beach, and we biked to the Mason-Dixon line, which was not far from our home.

As with most couples who have had the first child, Dorothea and I talked about having another baby, in spite of our poor finances, and finally made the decision to try in January of 1968. Kathryn was born at Wilmington General Hospital in October of that year.

Societal norms were rapidly changing, and it was becoming accepted that the husband support his wife in the pregnancy. I tried very hard to do what was expected of a sophisticated and progressive young man so we registered for Lamaze classes, and I signed up to be in the delivery room during Kathryn's birth, something quite unusual in 1968.

My experience in the delivery room was very interesting and a bit shocking, and how I got to participate is a story in itself. We were driven to the hospital by one of the acquaintances we made in the Lamaze class and, after registration, Dorothea and I were taken into a hospital room to wait for progress on the delivery. When it was time, Dorothea was taken into the delivery room and I was whisked off by a doctor into a locker room to change before going into the delivery room. This was a typical locker room, the type you would find in a gym or workout facility. I was told to get undressed and put on scrubs, with white but bloodied white Oxford shoes. This all seemed matter-of-fact to the doctor that was instructing me. During the delivery, when all was chaos, with a Doctor and two nurses rushing about, I was at Dorothea's head, talking with her, and remember seeing a bucket placed below her. Then came the sound of the snip of scissors and the indelible vision of what this meant. It quickly became obvious why the shoes were bloodied. The birth was quick, and I was very near fainting when Kathryn was born and placed in my arms. What an experience. I don't recall how I got home that night. I returned the next day to see our beautiful Kathryn.

I must mention one other incident that nearly cost our entire family our lives, although I still get goosebumps when I think of it. Just after Kathryn was born, I bought a used, barely-drivable, compact car, a Renault Dauphine, and we made plans to visit the Moons in Princeton that Thanksgiving Holiday, November 1968.

We set out on that rainy, misty morning with a packed car, loaded the two kids and various food dishes Dorothea prepared. While on Interstate 95, I lost control of the vehicle and we flipped over several times. It was a miracle we weren't killed.

Someone called the police and we were driven in a police car to a hospital. After the adrenaline of the event had worn off, I recall calling the Moons to tell them what had happened, but I was unable to get the words out. I was in shock and Dorothea had to finish the conversation. The Moons arrived the next day with the entire Thanksgiving Day dinner in tow. This event used up one of our nine lives.

Figure 41. Photo of Christine, Kathy and me in Newark Delaware a few months after Kathryn was born, most likely in December 1968.

Graduate School and Beyond, 1968-1969

By the winter of 1968, I had melted into the fabric of US society; feeling assimilated, having put my past behind me, or so I thought. I am not sure an immigrant ever feels assimilated. Can one really forget where they came from?

We moved to Ithaca in the winter of 1968; Frank and Lee returning to Newark to help us pack, and Frank and I driving a moving truck with Lee and Dorothea following us in their white Plymouth Valiant, whose floorboard was so rusted that you could see the road whizzing past, with three kids under the age of three. How we ever made it to Ithaca alive that winter is another miracle.

1968 was a tumultuous and turbulent year in the US. It was the year when student unrest precipitated national crises in Europe as well as the US, starting with sit ins on college campuses in Italy and France and developing into political terrorism in Europe, and protests in the US cities and college campuses. Terrorism perpetrated in the West German Republic by the Baader-Meinhof gang in West Germany, and riots on the campus of the University of Rome, spread to Columbia University, Kent State University where several students were killed by National Guard troops in May of 1970, and the 1968 Democratic National Convention in Chicago.

I started graduate work in January of 1969, Spring semester, just at the time when Richard Nixon was elected and the protests against the Vietnam War and the Civil Rights issues were reaching their peak. I came to realize that Cornell was an exclusive University that had many rich undergraduates with few being from New York, and most of my cohort of graduate student friends were from the Midwest or Northeast suburbia. Dorothea and I were still living on meager resources of a research stipend from the Materials Science Department and loans from the federal government and I was being swayed by the political events going on in the country. I came to think the Vietnam war was wrong and disagreed with the government position of sending troops to fight in a place where a number of my high school friends had died. Can you imagine watching the nightly news and hearing of daily casualty figures. It was very depressing. Even though I was against the war, I had also come to realize that I was naïve regarding the antiwar movement which had elements of socialism, Maoism and communism and was overtaking legitimate protest against the war. This was also the time of protest for civil rights. The protest for Civil Rights at Cornell culminated when black students barricaded themselves in the Student Union (Willard Straight Hall) and as they stood before the entrance to read their protest statement, showed themselves holding shotguns. This was shocking. Students held rallies on the Liberal Arts Quad, speeches were made and resolutions adopted, reminding me of what I had read of the French Revolution and the Reign of Terror. Some engineering students participated in this mayhem but not all were willing to risk everything, including getting arrested. I wanted this mayhem to stop. I had many arguments with my fellow graduate students regarding the war protests, burning of draft cards and the escape of some to Canada; I was on the liberal side of the antiwar argument at this time. But at the time of the takeover of the student union, I sensed the naivete of the student body in dealing with this threat of violence and I feared that this confrontation would lead to bloodshed. Luckily this did not happen and the university administration defused the situation. Somehow the university got back to normal; the Vietnam war began to wind down, and the flight to the moon and Watergate turned the nation's attention to other issues. As I've already said, the cultural changes during the Trump presidency are minor compared to what was going on in the late 60s. I show below a chart with some of those momentous events between 1968 and 1970.

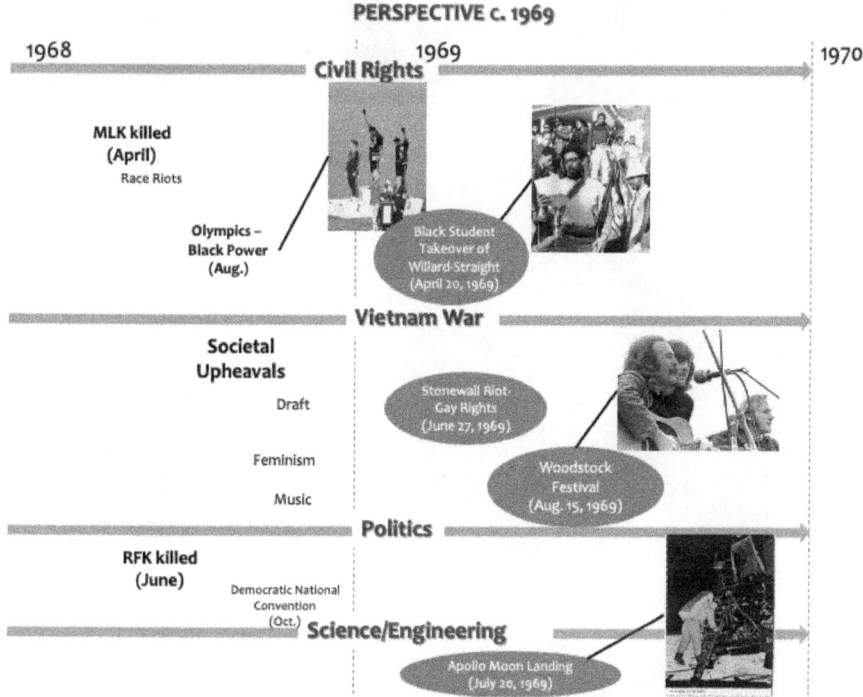

Figure 42. Time perspective of the years 1968 and 1969, showing some of the major events that went on at that time. A turbulent time in US history.

Afterword

I end this memoir in January of 1969, the year we arrived at Cornell and I began my studies for a PhD in Materials Science. It was during my time at Cornell that I came to examine my upbringing, of coming to grips with my immigrant life, my relationship with my mother and siblings, and nurturing my family. I had reached my goal, melted into the fabric of the US society, but now was unclear what this had gotten me. I slowly came to realize that you cannot escape your upbringing no matter how hard you try. In my case I had spent most of my formative years trying to do this by denying my Ukrainian heritage, escaping from the tiny enclave of my life, and getting lost in the US. I was reluctant to talk about my background but I came to re-embrace it as I began to mature.

I completed my PhD in 1973, accepted an offer of a job at Texas Instruments, Inc. and we headed via train to Dallas, the city where President Kennedy was assassinated. We stopped in Chicago to visit Mary, and I started work as a research engineer at Texas Instruments in Richardson, Texas in the Fall of 1973. I didn't like TI nor Dallas and told Dorothea that we would not stay there.

Steven Danyluk

My last 40 Years

I spent 32 years working as a professor in academic institutions, first at the University of Illinois at Chicago (13 years) then at the Georgia Institute of Technology (19 years). I moved jobs the first five years after receiving my PhD; first working at Texas Instruments (TI) a semiconductor manufacturer in Richardson, TX, and then at Argonne National Laboratory, a national nuclear facility about 20 miles southwest of Chicago, specializing in nuclear reactor research. I hated working at TI and Argonne and in 1980, I took a position as Associate Professor at the University of Illinois at Chicago (UIC), a job I loved and which, unforeseen by me, forced me back to my immigrant roots. I taught undergraduate and graduate courses in the Civil Engineering, Mechanics and Metallurgy Department, and I had US and foreign graduate students.

Chicago is the second or third largest city in the US, depending on how you count, it is multi-ethnic, multi-racial and full of students struggling to get a higher education. UIC was started as a commuter school as the University of Illinois, Navy Pier campus, in 1947, for returning veterans from World War II and eventually the campus was built at the center of the city, near Union Station, and renamed the University of Illinois, Circle Campus. The Circle Campus has an interesting history which you may want to read about. It was built with the support of mayor Richard Daley, who wanted a University of Illinois campus in the city, and in the 1980s, it's student body was composed of first generation students and immigrants looking to get a higher education. The campus merged with the medical college in the mid 1980s and changed its name to the University of Illinois at Chicago (UIC). Engineering is a small part of UIC, having approximately 100 faculty and 2,000 undergraduates at the time I was there, while the medical school is composed of a Nursing and Medical College, Dental school, and a hospital, these units much larger than the College of Engineering. Many of the engineering undergraduates were either immigrants or children of immigrants, and the graduate students were mainly foreigners who had come to know of Chicago over the decades as an entry point to the US. I came to like these students. I typically lectured on a junior level course in material science, which was required by all engineering students, 350 undergraduate students per class, and to smaller class sizes of approximately 20 graduate students. I'm sure they saw me as a typical, well-to-do American professor, not an immigrant like themselves, but with privileges that they didn't have access to. Some of the undergraduates got in academic trouble in their freshman year, got expelled, then tried to come back after learning from their mistakes. I remember these students very well. A number of them came to see me about a recommendation for readmission, promising that they had learned their lesson and would now study hard. Many times, I supported their readmission and these rehabilitated students did very well, and the ones that I supported graduated with honors.

 I invited some of these students to our home and over a number of years I instituted a practice of inviting graduate and undergraduate students to a local Pizza joint where I bought the drinks and we talked about their aspirations. I am proud to have supported their educations. I had many foreign students from Korea, China, Mexico, India, Singapore, and South America and I always enjoyed talking to them about their immigration experiences. Many of these students did not go back to their mother countries but were assimilated into the US. I continued my career at the Georgia Institute of Technology in January 1993, where I took a position of the Morris Bryan Jr. Chair in Mechanical Engineering, an endowed chair in the George Woodruff School of Mechanical Engineering. I was hired by Ward Winer, who at that time was the Chair of the Woodruff School and to who I owe my rise in status in the academic community. Georgia Tech is principally an engineering university situated in the middle of Atlanta, with an outstanding undergraduate student body. However, the graduate class was again made up of students from all over the world and I continued my conversations with these students of their immigrant experiences. I published lots of papers and have 9 patents to my credit, which you can look up on the internet, all done with the help of my graduate students. I continued to teach undergraduates and graduate students and retired in 2012. In all, I had supervised 29 PhD and 60 MS students throughout my career and a number of the research ideas formed the basis of three companies that I founded.

My greatest accomplishment is my family. To date, we have four grandchildren and three great grandchildren.

I hope that they have learned something of my background by reading this memoir: always look forward, don't be afraid of taking chances, and value your family.

Acknowledgements

Many of my family members helped with and supported this effort to write my history, and I cannot thank them enough for this support. I gratefully acknowledge the help of my wife Dorothea who encouraged me to keep going with this project when many times I thought I might quit. I would also like to thank Mary, Frank and Lee Moon, and Christine and Kathryn for editing and proofing the draft version of these memoirs. Their suggestions were critical to get this memoir in a readable form. The remaining mistakes are my own. Many of the details of the years before WWII were provided by Mary, with additional input from, Dmytro and Nick, who reminded me of the memories that I had since forgotten.

About the Author

Steven Danyluk was born in Schweinfurt, Germany, just after the end of WWII. He and his family ended up in a displaced persons camp in the American Sector. His father died in one of the camps during immigration processing. He arrived in the US in December 1950 in New York City and grew up there. He completed grade school in the Ukrainian section of lower Manhattan, went to high school in The Bronx, then left New York to complete his BS and PhD degrees at the University of Delaware and Cornell University. He was married to Dorothea in 1964 and they have two children, four grandchildren, and three great grandchildren, two of whom were born in 2020. He took a position in 1980 as professor at the University of Illinois at Chicago, and in 1993 as the Morris Bryan, Jr. Chair of Advanced Manufacturing at the George W. Woodruff School of Mechanical Engineering, and Director of the Manufacturing Research Center at the Georgia Institute of Technology. He is a widely-published author, graduated 29 PhDs and 60 MS students, has received 9 patents, and started three companies. He retired in 2012.

References

Ukraine, A History, Fourth Edition, Orest Subtelny, University of Toronto Press, 2009.

The Eagle Unbowed, Poland and the Poles in the Second World War, Halik Kochanski, Harvard University Press, Cambridge-Massachusetts, 2012.

Catherine the Great, Portrait of a Woman, Robert K. Massie, Random House, Inc., New York, 2011.

Memoirs of the Second World War, Winston S. Churchill, Houghton Mifflin Company, Boston, MA, 1959.

Treaty of Riga, Google search: ungarisches-institut.de/dokumente/pdf/19210318-1.pdf

Robert Oppenheimer: A Life Inside the Center, Ray Monk, Doubleday, N.Y. 2012.

The Harvest of Sorrow, Soviet Collectivization and the Terror-Famine, Robert Conquest, Oxford University Press, New York, 1986.

Savage Continent, Europe in the Aftermath of World War II, Keith Lowe, St. Martin's Press, New York, 2012.

The First World War, John Keegan, Vintage Books, a Division of Random House, New York, 1999.

Stories of Immigrant Life, 97 Orchard Street, New York, Lower East Side Tenement Museum, Linda Granfield with Photographs by Arlene Alda, Tundra Books, 2001.

The Beauty and the Sorrow, An Intimate History of the First World War, Peter Englund, Alfred A. Knoft, Publ, 2011.

Bloodlands, Europe between Hitler and Stalin, Timothy Snyder, Basic Books, 2010.

Strangers in the Wild Place, Adam R. Seipp, Indiana University Press, 2013

The Wild Place, Kathryn Hulme, Little Brown and Co., 1953

A Global Age, Europe 1950-2017, Ian Kershaw, Viking, Random House, 2018

Woodrow Wilson and World Settlement, Raymond Stannard Baker, Doubleday, Page and Company, New York, 1922.

Red Famine: Stalin's War on Ukraine, Anne Applebaum, Anchor Books, 2017.

George Marshall, Defender of The Republic, David L. Roll, Calliber 2019.

Savage Continent: Europe in the aftermath of World War II, Keith Lowe, St. Martins Press, 2012.

Hardhat Riot, Nixon, New York City and the Dawn of the White Working-Class Revolution, David Paul Kuhn, Oxford University Press, 2020.

CPSIA information can be obtained
at www.ICGtesting.com
Printed in the USA
FSHW010859160321
79522FS